WRITERS AND THEIR W

Isobel Armstrong
General Editor

Bryan Loughrey
Advisory Editor

D0231983

Emily Brontë

EMILY BRONTË

from the painting by BRANWELL BRONTË, *c 1833*
by courtesy of the National Portrait Gallery, London

Emily Brontë

Stevie Davies

Northcote House
in association with the
British Council

© Copyright 1998 by Stevie Davies

First published in 1998 by Northcote House Publishers Ltd, Plymbridge House, Estover Road, Plymouth PL6 7PY, United Kingdom.
Tel: +44 (01752) 202368 Fax: +44 (01752) 202330.

British Library Cataloguing-in-Publication Data
A catalogue record for this book is available from the British Library

ISBN 0-7463-0834-5

Typeset by PDQ Typesetting, Newcastle-under-Lyme
Printed and bound in the United Kingdom

for Lyndall Gordon
in friendship

Contents

Acknowledgements

I am deeply grateful to the staff at the Library of the Brontë Parsonage Museum, Haworth, for their help in the writing of this book, especially Ann Dinsdale, Assistant Librarian, and Kathryn White, Deputy Curator of the Museum. Their expertise was given with dashes of humour and always without stint.

I should also like to thank Jane Sellars, till recently Director of the Museum, for her help and friendship, and Judith Warner, the Parsonage Education Officer, whose knowledge and solidarity are greatly valued.

I thank Frank Regan for our ongoing conversation on Emily Brontë, on whose work he is, modestly but deeply, an expert; and for playing Hercules to free me for writing. Leon Stoger has explored with me the relationship between music and literature, and I record my gratitude for his insights. I thank Ann Mackay for her friendship and for ferrying me and my books to and from libraries. I am indebted to Patsy Stoneman for an exchange of truly stimulating ideas; to John Waddington-Feather for his writerly support, and to Edward Chitham for his characteristic generosity in sharing thoughts. I thank Frances Hill for her writerly solidarity and Joy Anderson for all that her friendship means to me.

I am grateful to my fellow-readers at the Centre for Continuing Education at Manchester University, especially Jo Bindley, Muriel Boroughs, Jo Crilly, Neil Gordon, Helen Hesford, Sheila Hilliard, Avril Ravenscroft, Priscilla Tolfree, and Barbara Wilson. Finally, I should like to acknowledge *my* Emily, who lives up to her namesake.

Biographical Outline

1818	Emily Jane Brontë born on 30 July 1818, at Thornton, Yorkshire, fifth of six children of Reverend Patrick Brontë, and Maria *née* Branwell, of Penzance.
1820	Anne Brontë, Emily Brontë's closest sibling-friend, born on 17 January. Family move to Haworth, West Yorkshire, where Patrick Brontë held Perpetual Curacy.
1821	Death of Emily Brontë's mother.
1824	Emily Brontë registered at Clergy Daughters' School, Cowan Bridge.
1825	Maria and Elizabeth Brontë, Emily Brontë's elder sisters, brought home from Cowan Bridge to die; Emily and Charlotte fetched home.
1826	Brother Branwell's acquisition of a set of toy soldiers from Leeds, source of Brontë children's secret plays, imaginary colonies, juvenilia, and the Gondal world Emily shared with Anne.
1833	Ellen Nussey's first visit to Haworth, in July.
1833 or 34	Acquisition of cottage piano.
1834	Emily and Anne Brontë's first diary paper.
1835	July–October: short-lived attempt to become pupil at Miss Wooler's School at Roe Head.
1837	June: second diary paper.
1838–9	Teaches at Law Hill, girls' school at Southowram, near Halifax.
1841	Third diary paper.
1842	Attends with Charlotte, Pensionnat Heger at Brussels as student of French, German, piano, and other subjects, February–November. Writes French essays,

including 'The Cat' and 'The Butterfly'. Returns at news of Aunt Branwell's death.

1844   Acquisition of eight-volume anthology of sheet music for piano, *The Musical Library*. Reading German. Probable acquaintance with works of Goethe and Schiller, and ideas of Berkeley and Schlegel. Writes 'To Imagination' and 'O thy bright eyes'.

1845   Fourth diary paper. Visits York with Anne Brontë. Dismissal of brother, Branwell, from post as tutor to Robinson family at Thorp Green for misconduct; Branwell's deterioration.

1846   Charlotte Brontë's discovery of Emily's secret cache of poetry results in publication of *Poems by Currer, Ellis and Acton Bell*, by Aylott & Jones, selling only two copies.

1847   Publication of Charlotte Brontë's *Jane Eyre* by Smith, Elder, in October; and of *Wuthering Heights* with Anne Brontë's *Agnes Grey*, in December.

1848   Death of Branwell from consumption, in September; death of Emily Brontë on 19 December, also from consumption. Publication of Anne Brontë's *The Tenant of Wildfell Hall*.

1849   Death of Anne Brontë, in May, at Scarborough, of consumption. Charlotte Brontë publishes *Shirley*, memorializing Emily and Anne Brontë.

1850   Charlotte Brontë edits new edition of *Wuthering Heights* and *Agnes Grey*, adding 'Biographical Notice', 'Editor's Preface', and 'Selections from Poems by Ellis Bell', rewriting the poetry to make it more conventionally acceptable.

Abbreviations and References

References to Emily Brontë's poetry are to *The Complete Poems of Emily Jane Brontë*, ed. C. W. Hatfield (New York: Colombia University Press, 1941).

AB	Anne Brontë
BE	Charlotte Brontë and Emily Brontë, *The Belgian Essays*, ed. and trans. Sue Lonoff (New Haven, Conn.: Yale University Press, 1996)
BEM	*Blackwood's Edinburgh Magazine*
BPM	Brontë Parsonage Museum
BST	*Brontë Society Transactions*
CB	Charlotte Brontë
CH	*The Brontës: The Critical Heritage*, ed. Miriam Allott (London: Routledge & Kegan Paul, 1974)
EB	Emily Brontë
EN	Ellen Nussey
G.	Elizabeth Gaskell, *The Life of Charlotte Brontë*, ed. Alan Shelston (Harmondsworth: Penguin, 1975)
JB	Juliet Barker, *The Brontës* (London, 1994)
L.	*The Letters of Charlotte Brontë*, i. *1829–47*, ed. Margaret Smith (Oxford: Clarendon Press, 1996)
LFC	*The Lives, Friendships and Correspondence of the Brontë Family*, ed. T. J. Wise and J. A. Symington (4 vols.; Shakespeare Head; Oxford: Basil Blackwell, 1933)
LG	*The Letters of Elizabeth Gaskell*, ed. J. A. V. Chapple and A. Pollard (Manchester: Manchester University Press, 1966)
MB	Maria Brontë
PB	Patrick Brontë
WH	Emily Brontë, *Wuthering Heights*, ed. Ian Jack with an introduction by Patsy Stoneman (Worlds Classics: Oxford: Oxford University Press, 1995)

1

A Question of Privacy

In the library of the Brontë Parsonage at Haworth is a drawer of objects never shown to the public, unless a curious scholar requests a personal viewing. Shrouded away from the common eye, which may rove at will over gauzy bonnets, Charlotte's headless dummy modelling a dress, or one and a half mouldered pattens belonging to Aunt Branwell, are seven pairs of stockings, plus an odd one, belonging to the Brontë sisters. The odd one is Emily's.[1]

One views the contents of this drawer with a mortified shiver of trespass, relieved to see it slide shut on its 150-year-old trove of used and useless hosiery. It is not just the fact that the stockings are plumped up with tissue paper, making the drawer seem inhabited by tiny legs, which so disquiets; but that these intimate garments bear stains and darns which their owners left in them. The preserved stockings (and apparently there is a corset of Charlotte's too, of minute dimensions) throw us back on questions of the wholesomeness of our curiosity; and upon the utter deadness of the Brontës. Nothing haunting here; nothing romantically secret in these yellowing revelations: but an exposure to a privacy, a reprimand to its violator. We are reminded of the reward of nosing too far into other people's dead business: carrion curiosity, pecking at the dead, denying their right to the permanent privacy of oblivion, scents its own corruption. As I turned away, the library took on, for a few minutes, a mortuary air. But when I opened a book, the living spoke to me.

How far should we delve into the life of artists? This is a pertinent question in an age when biography *sells*, and Brontë-mania is an industry. But didn't Charlotte, Emily, and Anne bring it all on themselves by writing so brilliantly of curiosity

1

and the desire to explore a private world? Hiding behind their Bell pseudonyms, they wrote their hearts out behind a screen, their seclusion generating the Bell-mania that hit London, with *Jane Eyre*, *Wuthering Heights*, and *Agnes Grey* in 1847. Who were they? How many – three, or one with three pen-names? What sex? Age? Guesswork commenced. Then in one year, 1848–9, three of the four Brontë siblings died, and the legend grew from their graves, fostered by the inconsolable Charlotte. Within six years Charlotte too had died and in 1857 Mrs Gaskell published her inflammatory biography, *The Life of Charlotte Brontë*, causing furore. The great northward trek began of pilgrims to the shrine. A museum; a literary society; mushrooming souvenir shops, tearooms, car parks, and Brontë walks; an industry, affording livelihoods to a community after the death of the textile mills.

Martha Brown, one of the Parsonage servants, seems to have received the stockings as mementoes. It was an age when retention or recycling of objects belonging to the dead did not seem morbid; part sentiment, part frugality, garments continued to do duty when the bodies had been cast off. As the sisters' legend grew, every meanest object became a relic, carrying a certain glamour and fascination. Furniture, pictures, ornaments, cups, books came back to source at the Parsonage, as if a magnet had pulled them together, against time's tendency to scatter and dissipate. Replacing the cup on the shelf, or Mr Brontë's spectacles on his opened bible, generated an odd sense that everything was in place for their return. The same magnet pulled us, readers and ramblers, to a consecrated space, both in the Parsonage and out on Penistone and Haworth moors, Top Withens, Ponden, scouting for the originals of fictional houses and moorlands readers had inhabited in imagination. The Parsonage became a reliquary, filled with venerated objects, of a potency and glamour beyond the retrieved lost property of young, impoverished gentlewomen hanging on to their respectability as the parson's children in a high economic gale.

Their father, eldest son of an Irish peasant farmer, had been born in 1777 in a two-room cottage in Drumballyroony-cum-Drumgooland, in County Down, Ulster. Intimate with poverty, he knew his daughters must be educated to earn their own living. Patrick had vaulted via Cambridge University from base origins to the respected clerical middle class, but in general disapproved of audacious mobility and wrote *Cottage Poems* (1811) in simple language to urge the poor to pious passivity. In 'The Irish Cabin', he paints an idealized picture of:

> A neat Irish cabin, snow proof,
>> Well thatched, had a good earthen floor,
> One chimney in midst of the roof,
>> One window, and one latched door.[2]

Of course one would not want it for oneself and one's own family – could not wait to escape over the water, even exalting his name from low Brunty or Prunty to the exotic Brontë, after Lord Nelson's Sicilian fiefdom, accolade of Imperial valour. Ex-Brunty, ex-Irishman, ex-peasant Brontë regarded himself as a prodigious exception to the rule. He was now in a position to advise the labouring poor of their privileged lot, for 'Your labours give the coarsest food, | A relish sweet: and cleanse the blood'. He imagined seraphic peasants, rather lean from lack of food but wholly Wordsworthian in spirit:

> Our peasant long was bred,
> Affliction's meager child,
> Yet, gratefully resigned,
> Loud hymning praises, smiled,
>> And like a tower
>> He stood unmoved,
>> Supported by
>> The God he loved.[3]

Patrick had an endearing tendency to overlook the sardonic source of his favourite allusions: it was rebellious Satan in Milton's *Paradise Lost*, a poem beloved by Patrick, who 'stood like a tower'.[4] Patrick blesses all such edifying peasants and the charity these have-nots draw from the haves. Having experienced the violence of civil conflict in the 1798 Irish rebellion and the Luddite riots in the West Riding in 1812, he shuddered at the memory all his life.

Maria Brontë, his wife, came from Penzance, a Cornish Methodist, and a woman of spirit, to judge from her love letters, a sheaf of which Patrick handed to Charlotte in adult life. Emily Brontë never knew of the existence of these letters, the vestige of a vanished beloved. Charlotte opened the pages with

3

a sense of poignant elation that some token had been preserved:

> the papers were yellow with time all having been written before I
> was born – it was strange to peruse now for the first time the records
> of a mind whence my own sprang – and at once strange and sad and
> sweet to find that mind of a truly fine, pure and elevated order...I
> wished She had lived and that I had known her.[5]

'The records of a mind' is a phrase that echoes as we read
Charlotte's account of reading her lost mother's voice back into
being. Maria left one unpublished literary work, 'The Advantages of Poverty in Religious Concerns'. Here she imagines the
rage of those who watch their children 'famishing with cold &
hunger'[6] while rich sots surfeit. But poverty is pietistically seen
by Maria as a vacuum into which Christian Charity rushes.
Squalour can edify the poor man by spiritualizing him and the
rich man by giving opportunity for Christian benevolence.
God's balance sheet ultimately equalizes credit with debit. Yet
when Maria came to die of stomach cancer in September 1821, at
the Parsonage, leaving a brood of six brilliant, needy children,
all under the age of 7, she failed to die an edifying death. Her
husband recorded with dismay that, though she attained
ultimate calm, hers had not been a model deathbed, for 'the
great enemy...often disturbed her mind in the last conflict'.
The nurse heard her shrieking, 'Oh God my poor children – Oh
God my poor children',[7] and perhaps she also blasphemed in
her agony, given the bedside presence of 'the great enemy' –
and perhaps her children (who went very quiet) overheard her.

She left an absence Emily sought all her life to recoup,
recapitulated by the deaths of the two elder Brontë sisters four
years later.

Meanwhile, the rent-free roof over the Brontë heads was as
perishable as Patrick's life. The Parsonage would have to be
evacuated by the daughters when he died. The Brontë young
grew up taking care of their belongings; they hoarded, patched,
turned, blackleaded the range, beat carpets, and baked bread;
they equipped themselves to go out to work as governesses or
teachers in an age when ladies did not. But ladies they were, as
daughters of the Evangelical perpetual curate, asserting his
authority in the pulpit, in his strange high-winged collar with
which he warded off draughts and germs.

Where's the collar? Few pretend much interest in Patrick's collar if we can spy on Charlotte's petticoat. For dead female celebrities, a special ghoulishness is reserved, whose intrusiveness owes much to sexual prurience. Charlotte knew they risked it, and that was what engendered the machismo swagger of those brawny pseudonyms: Currer, Ellis, and Acton Bell – memorably offbeat. They might have hidden more effectively behind Charles, Edward, and Andrew. But Charlotte was cross-biased by contrary needs: she half-wanted her incognito broken – to be known, and yet not known – celebrity on her own terms. And so she dashed impetuously to London in July, 1848, with Anne in tow, to blurt to her publisher that: 'We are three sisters', and George Smith, gallant, handsome, and 25, struggled to camouflage his half-amused incredulity at the myopic, tiny, shy but urgent woman and her reticent sister. Ellis, however, didn't go. And, livid to learn that his cover had been broken, subjected his fraternal colleague to a tempest of abuse. He refused to be known for a woman. If Charlotte quailed before the prospect of 'being made a show of – a thing I have ever resolved to avoid', Emily had never wanted anyone to see her private poems in the first place; had had them raided by Charlotte, was then steamrollered into publishing, and wrote a novel on the strict understanding that she was to remain incognito. Charlotte wrote to her publisher in a panic:

> Permit me to caution you not to speak of my Sisters when you write to me – I mean do not use the word in the plural. 'Ellis Bell' will not endure to be alluded to under any other appellation than the '*nom de plume*'. I committed a grand error in betraying his identity to you and Mr Smith – it was inadvertent – the words 'we are three Sisters' escaped me before I was aware – I regretted the avowal the moment I had made it; I regret it bitterly now, for I find it is against every feeling and intention of 'Ellis Bell'.[8]

Charlotte knew perfectly well Emily's phobia of being spied out by strangers, but in the drama of the moment had stampeded the prohibition. Yet nosy-parkering, Emily knew, was the very essence of literature. She was one herself, relishing village gossip. Without gossip, no stories. Without snooping, no secrets, to be kept or confided. She was mortally aware of the contrarieties of her position. Publication and notoriety inevitably opened her to the stare of the curiosity she had aroused.

5

Now that our eyes are everywhere, Emily is blessedly nowhere. The whole Parsonage is a series of memoranda that she once lived and that we have lost her. Emily is an especial magnet because of her cryptic, costive nature; saying nowt; keeping herself to herself. Emily-lovers abound, 150 years after her death: folk who feel a particular affinity with Emily, who 'know' her, see her ghost, or even mystically 'are' her. Emily and Death are commonly yoked together. Was she not romantically longing to die, was not her death a kind of suicide, they meditate? Bracing ripostes that she was a fit woman all her life, robustly avoiding 'poisoning doctors', who died of nothing more ethereal than tuberculosis, with acute diarrhoea, hardly seem to register. From the roped-off entrance to the dining room where the famous novels were probably written (the original table has now been acquired, with the letter 'E' scratched on to the polish), visitors are shown the sofa on which she died. Or rather, was supposed to have died. Juliet Barker (Director for many years, who ought to know (JB 576)) points out that there wasn't room for a lanky woman like Emily, at 5 foot 7 inches, to die on that cramped perch, given that her dog Keeper was observed to be lying beside her. But myths die harder than probabilities in these wuthering regions of the mind – most visitors continue to favour this theatre for her death scene.

At the centre of *Wuthering Heights*, there is a death scene whose equal for passionate theatricals only Shakespeare and the Renaissance dramatists offer. Yet nobody imagines Shakespeare died like Lear, or Webster like the Duchess of Malfi. The confusion of life with art has a peculiar force when it comes to the Brontës. This mental maelstrom is parodied by the erection in the Parsonage of the headstone of 'CATHERINE EARNSHAW LINTON' and 'HEATHCLIFF', relics of the Paramount film, either side of a door marked 'PRIVATE'.

The door marked PRIVATE leads to the library. I bare my shame by confessing that, after some hours of reading in the studious quiet, my eye strayed to the stocking drawer, which I asked to view a second time, in order to re-examine my feelings of prurience and revulsion. This time, however, I was balked: the drawer contained nothing more heinous than a line of aged legwear which should have been thrown away long ago. The relics – *mementi mori* – were inconsequent, the wearers safe from our rifling eyes.

Preserving and conserving were a passion of the culture in which the Brontës lived. Emily Brontë was a hoarder; she understood that instinct for keepsakes which recall lost times and people. In a piercing moment in *Wuthering Heights*, the narrator Ellen finds, at the moorland guidepost, 'a hole near the bottom still full of snail-shells and pebbles which we were fond of storing there with more perishable things' (*WH* 108); and 'sees' in her mind's eye, exactly as he was then, her early playfellow, the child Hindley, scraping out earth with slate, for the secret burial – and preservation – of their talismanic trove. While 'perishable things' have weathered away, these fragments of the eternal rocks beneath and the exoskeletons of their inhabitants endure in the hidden cache.

The older self finds the lost younger self – fleetingly – at this marker point. Burial, suggests *Wuthering Heights*, is not simply a matter of loss, but of arcane safe keeping. The graveyard of the chapel at Gimmerton Sough, resolving as it is into the moorlands, has strange preservative properties, sited 'near a swamp whose peaty moisture is said to answer all the purposes of embalming on the few corpses deposited there' (*WH* 21). *Wuthering Heights* is deeply concerned with a search for lost security, within a natural setting, in which earliest loyalties are most enduring. The moorlands are set before us as a creative and mysterious motherland which receives back its lost children and, in enigmatic form, preserves them. The novel is a testament that arouses readers to wonder, baffling us with the intimation of a secret, in which somehow we are all involved: 'surely you *and every body* have a notion that there is ... an existence of yours beyond you?' meditates Cathy (*WH* 81–2; emphasis added). Small wonder that, curiosity amounting to hunger aroused, 'every body' travels to the site of Emily's life and death, to find what if anything the house preserved of her.

Wuthering Heights is a snooper's charter. The narrator, Lockwood, prowls other people's secrets – a peeping Tom at a loose end in these (to him) strange northern regions. Barging into the centre of the centre, Cathy's boxbed, the narrator rummages a dead girl's book collection. Here he is impregnated with a dream which shows the universality of the novel's inmost tabooed recess. This dream of an icy girl-ghost, twenty years in exile, explodes into Lockwood's unconscious mind; the dream also bursts through into each reader's inmost self. This scene is amongst the most riveting and harrowing in the novel, as Lockwood (nice, polite young man) grinds the wraith's young wrist along the jagged glass.

> and rubbed it to and fro till the blood ran down and soaked the bed-clothes: still it wailed, 'Let me in!' and maintained its tenacious gripe, almost maddening me with fear. (WH 23)

The reader too is gripped and held: trauma becomes dream, which converts in turn to the reading experience; with the sense of a taboo transgressed, the deeply private made partially legible to electrified outsiders. Eye witness of Heathcliff's private 'agony', Lockwood turns away, wincing with voyeur's guilt, 'half angry to have listened at all' (WH 27).

How did Lockwood catch his dream? Through reading. Nosing around the handwritten diary of a dead girl, 'decypher[ing] her faded hieroglyphics' (WH 18), Lockwood was haunted by 'that minx, Catherine Linton, or Earnshaw, or however she was called'. No wonder that his attempt to erect a barricade *of books* against the revenant was abortive, the pyramid toppling inwards (WH 24). For they were Catherine's books, her outward mind.

How do we catch our dream of Emily Brontë? Originally, from reading. For reading can feel uncannily like a haunting, begetting the inner mind of the author on the deepest recesses of our own. I shall explore the idea that Emily imprints on the reader the literary version of what her characters undergo. We dream awake.

Dreams told many times over tend to lose their sense and spell. *Wuthering Heights* long ago entered a collective culture, to be dispersed at hundreds of removes from the original text, through films, operas, novels, ballets, musicals, popular songs, some (to be polite about it) closer to the text than others. These transmissions wander off into romance and enter into arranged marriage with commerce. There is not just gold but brass in 'the Brontës'. Millions who have not read the book have 'seen the film', which sends them tracking the memorials of a privacy. Off the beaten track as Haworth was, it is now a centre, with open doors at the Parsonage between 10 and 4, a time trap and time warp, promising to salvage the fascinating past from the deluge of time – a sandstone Ark, riding a sea of tombstones, on the crest of a cobbled hill.

Cameras snap everything in sight, from wooden posts to Branwell's local, the Black Bull. But from inside the house, the original view is occluded. From the front windows, Emily could see her father's Church of Saint Michael and All Angels (rebuilt in 1879); on the other she had a clear view (but the windows are now blocked off) of the open moors toward Brow Moor, Oakworth Moor, and Steeton Moor. Under the raucous disputes of the rooks in the seething trees, our lens is trained on a substituted view. Early photographs on display at the Parsonage show the churchyard much as it is now, but before the trees were planted to suck up the gaseous putrefaction from the corpses assembled, 44,000 of them – who once troubled the water supply with their emanations. Here and there a man in a topper poses, one foot on a slab, identity unknown.

This reminds us that the decade in which Emily Brontë was composing her novel was an age of new technology: the 'daguerreotype', earliest popular form of photograph, made its sensational début in English culture. A reprographic age set in. Louis Daguerre invented chemical processes to develop images, using mercury and silver oxide, with a fixative of hyposulphite of soda. This method soon found refinements, until, in the 1850s, a middle-class gentlewoman like Charlotte Brontë could leave her likeness in our hall on a *carte visite*. Suddenly, the passing moment could be fixed, suspended forever in all its immanence: a face, landscape, a battle, every kind of perishable. In 1843 Elizabeth Barrett wrote to her friend, mesmerized by the 'sense of nearness . . . the fact of the *very shadow of the person* lying there fixed for ever!'. She'd rather, she said, have 'such a memorial of one I dearly loved, than the noblest artist's work ever produced'.[9]

The phrase 'the very shadow of the person' gives pause. The word 'snapshot' was to be coined in 1860, crisply conveying the simultaneous liveliness and petrification of the event photographically reproduced. Such realism in the 1840s seemed magical, hypnotic: menacing to the livings of miniature- and portrait-painters. Paul Delaroche theatrically exclaimed: 'From today, painting is dead!' Some thought it 'not only impossible...but the mere desire alone... [is] blasphemy. God created man in his own image, and no man-made machine may fix the will of God.' A volume of *Blackwood's Edinburgh Magazine* which passed through Emily's hands scoffed at photography, which it compared with the hot-air balloon as a useless invention: 'we have but little hope of ever seeing anything tolerable from any machine. It must want colour...living expression...the play of features, which the pencil has the singular power of seizing and fixing; and its best likeness can only be that of a rigid bust, or a corpse.'[10]

To fix the fleeting and cull keepsakes from time was an obsession of that age: a new kind of colonization, of Time, now seemed feasible. The unphotographed universe lay all before them, a camera-taker's dream. The Brontë children were collectors, with investments in their past. Emily's scrupulously detailed portraits of her dog Keeper and her hawk, in pen and watercolour, show her own attempt to fix the loves of her life on paper. There are no photographs of Emily and her animals; we see her only in the moving oil painting from Branwell's damaged 'Gun group' and his less striking portrait of the sisters, with his own image scrubbed out as, presumably, unflattering. Yet our modern minds cannot help but function photographically: imagination replays the Brontë lives like a phantasmal film.

Emily's novel warns against the delusions of realism. The moors of *Wuthering Heights* are not verbal daguerreotypes of Haworth Moor, Dewsbury, Halifax, but the mindscape of their author, bearing private meanings, whose tracery of paths is a palimpsest of ways her mind has wandered. The novel is no postcard world of 'views' but an internalization of known spaces in a solipsistic cosmos. The difficulty of locating a path into this inner and recessive labyrinth is focused mockingly by *Wuthering Heights*, a novel almost irksome in its prescience of the obstacles to entry into the *terra incognita* of its author's mind.

Winter prevails at the story's advent, and with it cold ambivalence, darkness, and obliterated bearings for the book's confused narrator, our representative in this godforsaken back-of-beyond. What Lockwood needs, as he keeps telling his offhand hosts, is 'a guide', for the 'roads will be buried already'.

No reply. 'How must I do?' No reply. 'Do point out some landmarks,' he pleads, 'by which I may know my way home'. And he dreams of floundering through snowdrifts 'and Joseph for a guide. The snow lay yards deep...' (*WH* 21); dreams again, of an ice-cold child who has 'lost my way on the moor!' When he emerges into the snow-scene after his staggering night of disorientation, the landmarks have all come into doubt:

> the whole hill-back was one billowy, white ocean, the swells and falls not indicating corresponding rises and depressions in the ground – many pits, at least, were filled to a level; and entire ranges of mounds, the refuse of the quarries, blotted from the chart which my yesterday's walk left pictured in my mind.
>
> I had remarked on one side of the road, at intervals of six or seven yards, a line of upright stones, continued through the whole length of the barren: these were erected, and daubed with lime on purpose to serve as guides in the dark, and also when a fall, like the present, confounded the deep swamps on either hand with the firmer path: but excepting a dirty dot pointing up here and there, all traces of their existence had vanished; and my companion found it necessary to warn me frequently to steer to the right or left, when I imagined I was following, correctly, the windings of the road. (*WH* 29)

Here is a monochrome picture, amounting to photographic realism, of the contoured surface of the moors, bearing a visible remnant of 'a line of upright stones' to serve as landmarks across 'the barren'. Topography is totally known to the author, and there is nothing unaccountable in it: the narrator accounts matter-of-factly for the underlying structure of the ground (quarrying and pit refuse), measures with precision the space between markers ('six or seven yards') and can account for their phosphorescence as night-markers by noting that they have been lime-daubed. Emily Brontë's strict timekeeping and space-charting explain scenery as the residue of industrial activity. But mere appearances, the passage insists, are the height of treachery. The relation between visible surface and underlying landscape is arbitrary and variable, an anti-map which returns the picture imprinted on Lockwood's memory to a blank sheet 'blotted from the chart') in a sea of white. What guideposts have survived are cryptic and deranging, given the submergence of the majority, leaving a desystematized system of signs, no better than 'a dirty dot pointing up here and there' – illegible smudges

11

on a blank page. When abandoned by his companion in a safe area where 'I could make no error', Lockwood neatly manages to wander randomly 'sinking up to the neck in snow' (*WH* 29–30).

This description is itself a signpost to the reader, indicating a hazardous alienation between sign and meaning in *Wuthering Heights*, a book whose meanings are reclusive and aberrant. Dubious narrators give us directions leading straight to the literary equivalent of Joseph's 'bog-hoile'. We might extend the warning to the territory of the biographer. The leavings of a life – its 'memorials' – are commonly read as signposts guiding us through its journey. In the case of an author like Charlotte Brontë, who left copious memorabilia, in the form of personal letters, jottings, juvenilia, to lay alongside her works, we presume the guideposts to be meaningful. Try finding Emily Brontë with the few 'dirty dots' time has left us, and you are soon up to your neck in snow and feeling that the trail is very cold indeed. She was a person inscrutable even to her nearest kin, who said very little to anyone beyond her family. Emily wrote only three known letters to outsiders, curt missives – or dismissives – one of which (to Ellen Nussey, to whom she had no objection), concludes that she will get Anne to 'write you a proper letter – a feat that I have never performed' (L. 319). And don't expect me to start *now*, she intimates. Her life was led in the regions of the unsaid.

Emily's recorded remarks are alike defensively negative and laconic. To the wittering schoolgirls of Law Hill, Halifax, she confided her preference for the house dog over anyone else on the premises; at Brussels, when teased about her outlandish get-up, she retorted that 'she wished to be as God made her'. When Mary Taylor declared that she'd told so-and-so that religious belief was a matter 'between God and me' and no one else's business, Emily, who had hitherto been lounging mute on the hearth-rug, said 'That's right' (*LFC* i. 137). If these are guideposts, they all represent keep-off signs to trespassers.

Other guides (or 'dirty dots') are provided by the testimony of observers who came into contact with Emily Brontë. What did people make of this reserved, rigidly white-faced, silent young woman, when she made her sorties away from the privacy of 'the barren' to the loquacious society beyond? She left home on only four major occasions: for the Clergy Daughters' School at Cowan Bridge at the age of 6; to school at Roe Head in her late teens; as teacher at Law Hill at 20; nine months in Brussels in her mid-twenties, as student at the Pensionnat Heger.

Mrs Gaskell went searching for clues within a decade of Emily's death, but by this time a complex legend had already set in, and what she was able to detect had an ironic contradictoriness in keeping with a sign-system of 'swells and falls *not indicating* corresponding rises and depressions in the ground'. Mrs Gaskell was dismayed to encounter the shade of a rather nasty person, contradicting Charlotte's insistence that Emily was 'genuinely good, and truly great.' Mrs Gaskell kept that in quotation marks, for, as she frankly admitted, 'all that I, a stranger, have been able to learn about her has not tended to give either me, or my readers, a pleasant impression of her' (G. 379). Women were bred and educated to please. But Emily Brontë had impressed others with her unpleasantness and bad manners, it seemed.

How could nice Mrs Gaskell square this odious anomaly with the heroine Charlotte revered?

A difficult conundrum, since Charlotte's private opinion was that her sister ('Mine bonnie love' as she was) was impossibly perverse and cussed. And had a violent temper. When Emily lay dying, Charlotte warned against offering her medical advice:

> It is best usually to leave her to form her own judgment, and *especially* not to advocate the side you wish her to favour; if you do, she is sure to lean in the opposite direction, and ten to one will argue herself into non-compliance.[11]

Charlotte describes Emily as if she were a wilful child, who has to be humoured or manipulated. Every discussion became a battle for control; and Charlotte showed a desire to control her beloved sister in the measure that her sister resisted it. When Emily was dead, and could not answer back, Charlotte was free to dream up another Emily, whom she enshrined in her grief-stricken novel, *Shirley*.

Elizabeth Gaskell invested in Charlotte's myth, by weaving a tissue of anecdote that exalted Emily as a powerful genius who stood as an honourable exception from feminine norms. One might be forgiven for bringing away from Mrs Gaskell's *Life of*

Charlotte Brontë the notion that Emily spent much of her life involved in dogfights, beating up her dog Keeper for sullying the white counterpane until 'the half-blind, stupefied beast' was pounded into submission; breaking up a canine scrap with a pepperpot; cauterizing a dog-bite, feared to be rabid, with a red-hot iron. Imagine what palpitations Mrs Gaskell would have suffered, had one of her own nice, house-trained daughters engaged in pitch battle with a 'great dog, half mastiff, half bulldog, so savage'. Emily was a proven genius, and, further, a dead and buried genius, who was also a legend. So her aberrations could be defined as heroism. Elizabeth's description of the fight between Emily and Keeper is the war of domestic Titans:

> Charlotte saw Emily's whitening face, and set mouth, but dared not speak to interfere; no one dared when Emily's eyes glowed in that manner out of the paleness of her face, and when her lips were so compressed into stone. She went upstairs, and Tabby and Charlotte stood in the gloomy passage below, full of the dark shadows of the coming night. Down-stairs came Emily, dragging after her the unwilling Keeper, his hind legs set in a heavy attitude of resistance, held by the 'scuft of his neck', but growling low and savagely all the time...She let him go, planted in a dark corner at the bottom of the stairs; no time was there to fetch stick or rod, for fear of the strangling clutch at her throat – her bare clenched fist struck against his red fierce eyes, before he had time to make his spring, and, in the language of the turf, she 'punished him' till his eyes were swelled up, and the half-blind, stupefied beast was led to his accustomed lair. (G. 269)

Emily's compulsively violent behaviour is endowed with mythic vitality: her eyes 'glowed' and her lips compressed 'to stone' – recalling elemental fire at the Heights and the stone of the moorlands. You feel Mrs Gaskell giving her novelistic talents free rein, as she paints the stairwell into a theatre of shadows, in preparation for the fight. Picturesque idiom ('scuft of the neck') adds piquancy, like pickle to a sandwich, as Mrs Gaskell savours the scene. The device of inversion ('No time was there...') lets us know the literary crisis is upon us, and a volley of adjectives ('her bare clenched fist', 'his red fierce eyes') unleashes the contest. 'In the language of the turf', says Mrs Gaskell, changing metaphor and strategy, 'she punished him'; the cant of a male sports world seeks to normalize Emily's pathological ferocity. Mrs Gaskell hurries on to reassure her reader that Emily went on to soothe and medicate the swollen eyes of 'the...beast'. So that was all right then.

But was it? To me this guidepost looks like a 'dirty dot' in every sense, badly smudged and then doodled with to represent a star. The integrity of these shaggy-dog stories stands in doubt.

The more closely you study the anecdotes clustering around Emily, the more unsafe seems the ground. Take John Greenwood's description of Papa teaching his daughter to shoot:

> if he called upon her to take a lesson, she would put all down; his tender and affectionate 'Now my dear girl, let me see how well you can shoot to-day' was irristable [sic] to her filial nature, and her most winning and musical voice would be heard to ring through the house in response, 'Yes, papa'... She knew she had gratified him, and she would return to him the pistol, saying 'load again papa,' and away she would go to the kitchen, roll another shelful [sic] of teacakes, then wiping her hands, she would return again to the garden, and call out, 'I'm ready again, papa.' And so they would go on until he thought she had had enough practice for that day. 'Oh!' he would exclaim, 'She is a brave and noble girl. She is my right-hand, nay the very apple of my eye.'[12]

What a hectic life of hurtling between target practice and teacake duties is revealed here. The duteous maiden obedient to the patriarch's 'tender and affectionate' call to arms is also sublimely attached to those teacakes and the feminine indoor world they represent. Papa's concluding speech has a berserk sentimentality and a staginess ('Oh!', 'nay') suggestive of amateur theatricals or charades, staged within Greenwood's imagination, acting on some glimpse or phrase caught on the wing. Gun-toting Emily is positioned for the reader in a complex space between genders: as a genius, she is permitted to wield a gun, symbol of male power and predominance, but only in token of her *daughterliness* (unquestioning obedience to father's wishes). Probably, if left to her own devices, Greenwood's Emily would have indulged her supernatural passion for baking but father's will prevailed.

We can derive from these tales the general facts of Emily Brontë's physical courage, her handiness with firearms, an affinity with animals, a violent streak, and the tendency to act in a manner construed as 'male' rather than 'female'. The qualities on display in Gaskell and Greenwood being bullish rather than bovine, are felt to require adjustment.

Elizabeth Gaskell crossed the Channel in the early summer of 1856 and interviewed Constantin Heger, obtaining a report which is often uncritically quoted in its totality. Here, it is assumed, is a stable and reliable guidepost, magisterial, insightful, the opinion of a brilliant educator. To my jaundiced eye, Heger's assumptions look nearly as twaddling as Greenwood's. On 15 February 1842 Charlotte and Emily were received at the Pensionnat Heger in the rue d'Isabelle, Brussels. They had come to acquire a superior knowledge of French, German, music, and other subjects, as a preparation for securing financial independence by opening a school in England. The first thing Emily did, according to Charlotte, was to dispute the headmaster's teaching methods with him in a spirit of angry uncooperativeness, as he laid out to them his programme of studies. She 'said she saw no good to be derived from it' (study and emulation of literary models), and that 'by adopting it, they would lose all originality of thought and expression. She would have entered into an argument on the subject, but for this, M. Heger had no time' (G. 231). No time in both senses, I imagine. Cock-of-the-walk in this hen-coop of *mademoiselles*, Heger had probably never been taken on by a truculent female on a matter of principle in his life. A lean, scraggy, morose woman with no real command of the French language is dragged hundreds of miles across Europe by her sister's elated 'wish for wings...such an urgent thirst to see – to know – to learn', to one of the cultural capitals of Europe.[13] Immediately she takes her 'master's' teaching methods by the scruff of the neck and shakes them contemptuously. Not only did she protest but she wouldn't pipe down ('She would have entered into an argument...') and Heger put an abrupt end to the interview. Charlotte wrote ruefully that Emily and he 'don't draw well together at all'. Nevertheless, Emily 'works like a horse' (L. 285).

Meanwhile, Heger, liberal and paternalistic, though (according to the older sister) despotic and whimsical, a touch condescending, flirtatious with favourites, caught glimpses of the shy pair walking in the grounds, the tall and argumentative woman clinging desperately to her tiny elder, bearing down with her whole weight. What he saw was a picture of everything one deplored in a woman: 'egotistic and exacting,' Emily exerted 'unconscious tyranny' over the more pliable Charlotte.

What then of Emily's mental powers? Formidable, Heger assured Elizabeth Gaskell. What he told her was this: 'Emily had a head for logic, a capacity of argument, unusual in a man, and rare indeed in a woman.' How far can a reader trust the judgment of a man so abysmally sunk in the mire of misogyny and the nearby swamp of platitude? Heger's pat of praise swipes its object a back-handed blow. Is it possible that the *maître's* own 'head for logic' (like the culture that bred it) left something to be desired? His testimonial goes on:

> Impairing the force of this gift, was her stubborn tenacity of will, which rendered her obtuse to all reasoning where her own wishes, or her own sense of right, was concerned. 'She should have been a man – a great navigator,' said M. Heger in speaking of her. 'Her powerful reason would have deduced new spheres of discovery from the knowledge of the old; and her strong, imperious will would never have been daunted by opposition or difficulty; never have given way but with life.' And yet, moreover, her faculty of imagination was such that, if she had written a history, her view of scenes and characters would have been so vivid, and so powerfully expressed, and supported by such a show of argument, that it would have dominated over the reader, whatever might have been his previous opinions, or his cooler perceptions of its truth. (G. 230–1)

Heger's praise is circuitous rebuke. There was something skewed about her ('Impairing the force...'). Badly skewed, since it rendered her impervious to instruction. The problem was 'her stubborn tenacity of will': nothing wrong with her reasoning powers, but pig-headed.

How then could this obstinately self-assertive logician's fault (that of sticking to her own opinion and arguing it through) have been corrected? Heger's brainwave reveals the rift in his own mentality, without saying much worth hearing about Emily: 'She should have been a man.' Had she been of the right sex, her strength of character would have been normalized and sanctioned. The gander struts his philosophical stuff while the dun goose looks on and feebly quacks her admiration. But Emily's qualities were all gander and hence redundant. As a man, she could have been 'a great navigator'. Over the horizon appears the Emily-myth, all sails flying, a machismo dream of *Veni, Vidi, Vici*.

Being a woman, Emily was denied this ganderish destiny, and had to be a misfit instead, Heger implied. Yet Emily had long thought of herself as just that – a great navigator, explorer of new-found lands, sailing to her imaginary world of Gondal by the force of pure *jeu d'esprit*. We may recall the juvenile game of the Brontë children hatched in 1826 when Papa brought Branwell the twelve toy soldiers home from Leeds, 'the Twelves', who were also pioneers, waving their Union Jacks as they walloped the Dutch on Ascension Island and, landing on the shores of Ashantee, explored the interior of Africa, to found Glasstown. While Branwell's chief man was Buonaparte, Emily's was Sir William Parry, the Arctic explorer who, with Anne's man, Sir James Ross, had lately returned from expeditions to discover the North-West Passage. Parry–Emily and Ross–Anne went on to found their own imaginary country, known only to the two of them.

She had pursued the seafaring image in her poetry, with a dashing and jaunty air:

> I will be an Ocean Rover,
> I will sail the desert sea.
>
> ('O between distress and pleasure' (1839))

And sky-scanning at nightfall brought a sense of astronomical voyaging into the immune immensity of the world beyond our tainted globe:

> While gazing on the stars that glow
> Above me in that stormless sea.
> I long to hope that all the woe
> Creation knows, is held in thee!
>
> ('How clear she shines' (1843))

Sea-roving was a Romantic theme, in popular song and ballad. Emily owned Cramer's piano arrangements of 'The Stormy Petrel... And THE SEA ROVER'. She linked the poet-as-mariner motif with the poet as sky-traveller:

> I was at peace, and drank your beams
> As they were life to me

And revelled in my changeful dreams
Like petrel on the sea.

Thought followed thought – star followed star
Through boundless regions on,
While one sweet influence, near and far,
Thrilled through and proved us one.

('Ah, why because the dazzling sun' (1845))

These imaginative soul-journeys represented the side of Emily that Heger never saw; no one did but Anne. The front shown to Heger was distraught but controlled, pugilistic; it stated at every point, *Non serviam*. The poems, with their often moving tenderness, represent a vision whose integrity depended on intact privacy. To glimpse the Unseen, you must yourself be invisible. Their existence depended on blocking Heger out as a representative of a 'dark world' in which she was a pariah. In 1841 the Gondal princes and princesses were described as holed up in 'the palaces of Instruction'; their keepers, who had to be constantly outwitted and given the slip, were known as 'the Guardians'. This word had an interesting diversity of reverberations at this time. The 1834 Poor Law Act appointed a Board of Guardians to govern the detested workhouses; the word also signified one who has custody of an infant or idiot; a tutor. Emily saw herself at any educational establishment in the posture of Milton's Samson: 'Eyeless in Gaza at the mill, with slaves'. Heger and all other Guardians held the intellect hostage at the palace of Instruction, attempting to brainwash you with cant. Heger interpreted what she showed him in terms of what he was able to imagine. He invented a male Emily-navigator standing heroically at the bridge piloting his crew into peril.[14]

Mrs Gaskell did not think this odd at all. Warming to his frankness and charm, she found the trans-sexual fantasy of machismo all very right and proper.

Or, continued Heger, she might have been an historian. Her interpretations would have 'dominated over the reader' and convinced him of the rightness of her opinions (which were, however, wrong). Dangerous gifts, one would think. The navigator is heading straight for an iceberg and the historian is guiding a credulous readership straight for the rocks of error.

19

As it was, Emily was just a cantankerous, outspoken female, with a useless gift. All Heger's remarks contained awareness of the focused challenge made by his pupil's baleful power to his authority and to authority in general, between teacher and pupil, male and female, senior and junior.

Heger's testimony was given, of course, after Emily had passed out of his ken, into celebrity and early death. What he had observed at the time, out of the corner of his busy eye, had magnified with hindsight into a prediction of genius-to-be. The self-centredness he deplored was indeed the core of Emily's gift. She meant to be a vagrant Ulysses on her own odyssey, rather than plying the distaff with Penelope, and knew from her earliest days the unfeminineness of this going-it-alone. Her father acquired two years after her birth Hannah More's *Moral Sketches*, which referred women to Homer's *Iliad* for 'pictures of female excellence and domestic virtue'; called upon them not to 'desert their proper sphere... Why roam in useless and eccentric wandering?'; 'Our greatest danger begins from the moment we imagine we are able to go alone'. This latter sentiment has been underlined in strenuous pencil by Papa, Mama, or Aunt.

Heger, to his credit, fostered Emily's gifts as writer and musician, and as I shall show, the French essays she wrote in Brussels and the German and music she studied there are valuable resources for a reader puzzling how to link the frankly childish material of her diaries with the grandeur of *Wuthering Heights*. The 'dirty dots' begin at this stage to resemble musical notes and the old German script: they lead from Haworth and Gondal, through Brussels to Europe and back, and thence to *Wuthering Heights*.

Emily must have taken her studies at Brussels with desperate seriousness, for she antagonized not only her master but her pupils through her single-mindedness. Laetitia Wheelwright never forgave the odious Emily for her meanness to her three youngest sisters. She made the little ones cry by refusing to teach them during school hours 'as she would only take them in their play hours, so as not to curtail her own school hours'.[15] She had this one chance to master the world of knowledge for herself and she would seize it with both hands, stamping on the toes of 7 and 10 year olds who would never make anything of their minds, if need be. The great navigator had not a jot of feminine sympathy for her blubbering tutees, who preferred romping to tonic sol fa. Her nastiness seems to have been so democratically distributed that we can lean on it as solid and invariable: except for one guidepost deviating from all the others, about which, however, nothing much can be said.

This is Louise de Bassompierre: a 16 year old who was the only discoverable ex-pupil to have preferred Emily to Charlotte. Emily seems to have reached out in one-off friendship, giving her a signed pencil drawing of a storm-damaged pine tree. We know nothing further about the relationship. Like a solitary guidepost, apparently way out of line with the rest, it reminds us to suspect the view time has left us, as limited and random.

Given the scarcity of intelligible landmarks, how do we find the right hypotheses or pick the relevant from the agglomeration of Brontë irrelevancies? An account of Emily which omitted to name 'Gondal' would be outlandish. Yet how to link this imaginary world with *Wuthering Heights* is a conundrum that has defeated (whether they admit it or not) generations of sleuths. Gondal's genesis was in that 'web of sunny air' recalled with aching nostalgia by Charlotte in her poem 'Retrospect'. But the childish weaving of shimmering imaginings seemed to the older Charlotte to have rotted with time, as its child-explorers departed from source.

Emily's first diary paper of 1834 notes that 'The Gondals are discovering the interior of Gaaldine. Sally Moseley is washing in the back kitchen.' Amongst laundry smells and apple pudding to come, and Tabby, the servant, irked at being jabbed in the face by Emily's pen ('Ya pitterpottering there instead of pilling a potate'), the buccaneering pitter-potterers catch the giggly, humdrum reality of a kitchen and house humming with quotidian life – and the Gondal underworld simmering all the while. Emily seems a young 16; she seems even younger as a 27-year-old, in the last diary paper. The 1845 diary records a jaunt by herself and Anne to York, spending two nights away in a city whose historic walls, river, Minster, monuments, apparently failed to impress Emily, for

> during our excursions we were, Ronald MacElgin, Henry Angora, Juilet Augusteena, Rosabella Esmalden, Ella and Julius Egremont, Catherine Navarre and Cordelia Fitzaphnold, escaping from the palaces of instruction to join the Royalists who are hard driven at

present by the victorious Republicans... We intend sticking by the rascals as long as they delight us, which I am glad to say they do at present.

Anne, after the humiliated grind of governessing at Thorp Green, watching her brother degenerate, differed: 'The Gondals in general are not in first-rate playing condition. Will they improve?' She had outgrown make-believe and perhaps found her role as half a travelling troupe of players performing their private and impromptu theatricals all the way to York and back an embarrassment. Anne had already begun to write sober realism. Emily's defiant childishness in espousing 'the rascals' seems regressive, retrogressive. How do we make the quantum leap from Gondal to the Heights, in the novel published only two years later?

Perhaps Emily's part in the Gondal saga was *not* in fact as childish as the diaries imply. In the Gondal literature she must surely have honed a style and multivalent narrative method. But it has all vanished. Brontë precocity as practised by Branwell and Charlotte was hoarded in mountains of juvenilia, much of it in miniscule script in hand-made books, 1½ by 2 inches, sewn into covers made of sugar bags, parcel-wrappings, and wall-paper scraps. Charlotte preserved it carefully. Much of her juvenilia, is, candidly, juvenile. Perhaps Emily's wasn't. We shall never know because, apart from the poems which she transcribed in one of two notebooks, labelled 'Gondal Poems', the whole corpus of narrative, drama, annals, fictional journalism, maps, epistles, or whatever else documented those fabulous lands has been annihilated. Whether Anne or Emily, or (more likely) Charlotte after their deaths, burned or jettisoned it, Gondal, the creation of its founding mothers over two decades, was abolished in a matter of minutes.

Whatever you make of the York excursion in which we get our final glimpse of Gondal, you come away with the impression of a young woman in the halest of health. The myth of a wasting sufferer only ever half in this world can be firmly discountenanced. Like Catherine Earnshaw, she must have been 'a stout, hearty lass'. She was described as 'slouching around' on the moors, limbs 'loose and boyish'[16] beneath the limp skirts she wore, perhaps for freedom of movement. *Boyish?* The word fits in with the 'tomboy-as-genius' refrain which sounds throughout the record. Athleticism, fleetness of foot, and bounding energy were culturally constructed as male, not female. Ellen Nussey left some carefully crafted memoirs of Charlotte, Emily, and Anne which we need to consider seriously. She visited the Parsonage first when Emily was in her mid-teens, reserved indoors, but boisterous and carefree outside, according to Ellen. Tenaciously loyal friend to Charlotte, Ellen had neither the Brontë magnitude of aspiration, intellectual audacity, nor their feet-off-the-ground emotionalism. Ellen impresses us with her ordinariness; a kind of sane sentimentality characterizes her memoir of her visit. She recalls their walks out together, and how they called themselves 'the quartette', and clustered at a spot christened 'The Meeting of the Waters', a 'small oasis of emerald green turf, broken here and there by small clear springs.'

The quartette: years after their deaths, we feel Ellen nudging into the group, yearning to belong as a fourth Brontë. Ellen considered herself custodian of the Brontë memory; fought Charlotte's husband tooth and nail to show the reality of *her* friend (not *his* wife), by publishing letters which would show Charlotte in the light of 'a Christian heroine' (*L.* 38). How fit was Ellen Nussey to record the Brontë reality?

How competent is Ellen Dean in *Wuthering Heights* to gloss the seismic story?

Sequestered at 'The Meeting of the Waters', a murmur of girls accompanies the remembered purl of the stream. Here, Ellen cannot help covertly boasting 'we were hidden from all the world', one would-be Brontë in a huddle with three giggling intimates: 'we laughed and made mirth of each other, and settled we would call ourselves the quartette.' She emphasizes, with allowable hyperbole, the Brontë sisters' attachment to 'every moss, every flower, every tint and form', and singles out Emily's lanky, rangy freedom of movement and love of nature: 'Emily especially had a gleesome delight in these nooks of beauty.'[17] Ellen has rather a genius for hitting on exactly the wrong word: Emily might have blenched at wearing that epithet 'gleesome' like a jolly hat, and winced at cosy 'nooks of beauty'.

Ellen's description unconsciously owes much to sentimental songs of the period, especially Thomas Moore's 'The Meeting of the Waters'. Ellen's collection of sheet music is extant at the Parsonage, comprising easy ballads, pious pieces, and lugubrious dirges concerning dead babes or dead mothers. Ellen was a model of the genteel provincial *bourgeoise* in her elementary accomplishments. 'The Meeting of the Waters' occurs as a setting in Ellen's book, the accompaniment to the warbled text to be rendered 'Andante with expression':

> There is not in the wide world a valley so sweet
> As that vale in whose bosom the bright waters meet.
> Oh! the last rays of feeling and life must depart,
> Ere the bloom of that valley shall fade from my heart.
>
> (repeat)
>
> 'Twas that friends, the belov'd of my bosom, were near,
> Who made ev'ry dear scene of enchantment more dear,
> And who felt how the best charms of Nature improve
> When we see them reflected from looks that we love.[18]

Presumably Ellen could have chosen many other details from her memory: what might have prompted her allusion to 'The Meeting of the Waters', which she would certainly have expected readers to know by heart, as an old favourite? Surely there is a subliminal advertisement to readers to acknowledge Ellen herself as one of the 'friends, belov'd of my bosom' who endeared the spot to the Brontë 'quartette'? Beneath the song in Ellen's music book unscrolls the following delicious rhapsody:

MAZAWATEE TEAS RECALL THE DELICIOUS TEAS OF 30 YEARS AGO

Axiomatically, the tea of yesteryear was more delicious than today's; the turf of long ago more 'emerald'; bosom friends were, with hindsight, less chattery and inconsequent and more deeply intermingled; and a genius-to-be was not a queer fish but a reserved but romping lass with 'a lithesome, graceful figure', 'very beautiful eyes – kind, kindling eyes'. Ellen's most passionately genuine memories constantly turned, in the moment of recall, to platitude. Ellen's memories as recorded in *Scribner's Monthly* in 1871 had been a quarter of a century fixing; and the fixative was the stuff of Ellen Nussey's own consciousness.

Underneath it all, she is saying, Emily Brontë was a lissom, shy, nature-loving girl with beautiful eyes, somewhere between dark grey and blue, 'they varied so' (but she did not often look at you), one of whose 'rare expressive looks was something to remember through life, there was such a depth of soul and feeling' (but you hardly ever got one). 'She talked very little'.

This at least seems more certain than the flavour of Mazawattee tea, brewed in warm reminiscence.

But several flashes of recall bear signs of actuality. Ellen felt that Emily tolerated her because she took no notice of Emily's peculiarities. When she and Emily went on a joint ramble, Charlotte waited on tenterhooks, lest her sister had undertaken to appal their guest: 'And Emily, how did she behave?' Ellen reported that Emily was fond of luring Charlotte into proximity to animals known to frighten her sister, laughing at her phobia. This is presented as girlish teasing, but implies sharper hostility.

The most suggestive detail, however, is Ellen's remembrance that Emily and Anne went everywhere literally linked together: 'She and Anne were like twins – inseparable companions, and in the closest sympathy', 'always together and in unison like dearly attached twins', wandering around 'twined' in one another's arms 'whenever' not otherwise occupied. For Ellen, this closeness seems sweet and idyllic. One might wonder. Given the cloven pair-bond between Catherine and Heathcliff in *Wuthering Heights*, with its perilous and needy insecurity, such union might constitute a bereavement-in-the-making. The glimpses of Emily's and Anne's inturned relationship, conspiratorially murmuring to one another rather than addressing others, suggests a bonding common in identical twins, though there were eighteen months and a striking temperamental difference between them. Their lives and works were to cleave radically apart, Anne's strenuous and clement Christianity colouring her feminism, and leading her to dissent, in *The Tenant of Wildfell Hall* (1848), from *Wuthering Heights*. Ellen's celebration of their 'twinning' and 'twining' belongs to their mid-teens.

However, Ellen also recalls Emily sounding off opinions and speculations in an unentwined state: 'Emily, half reclining on a slab of stone, played like a young child with the tad-poles in the water, making them swim about, and then fell to moralising on the big and the little, the brave and the cowardly, as she chased them with her hand' (*L.* 599). This memory reverberates with major themes in Emily's poetry, essays, and novel. An amateur zoologist (and zoology at the humblest and most exalted levels was still at this time a branch of natural theology), she examines the behaviour of creatures in their habitat, when faced with a perceived threat. She notes two distinct kinds of tadpole behaviour, corresponding to flight and fight. The image of Emily here is in compellingly sharp visual focus, as she leans on one elbow, free hand churning the water. It is a description of a relaxed body and an alert mind, which moves from play to speculation. Power and fitness to survive were topics of fascination to her as a writer. Her bias toward 'the brave' over 'the cowardly' was a tendency she seems to have striven to correct, as in the Gondal debate-poem of 1839, 'Well, some may hate'. A sneering voice moves from pity to condemnation after the death of a base human specimen; finally it adjusts itself thus:

> Do I despise the timid deer
> Because his limbs are fleet with fear?
> Or would I mock the wolf's death-howl
> Because his form is gaunt and foul?
> Or hear with joy the leveret's cry
> Because it cannot bravely die?
>
> No! Then above his memory
> Let pity's heart as tender be...

To prefer the strong over the weak is blind prejudice, the voice tells itself, since species and individuals obey the laws of their own natures, and can do no otherwise. Emily Brontë would grasp the continuum on which humans and animals lived; the conflict of fit and unfit specimens, both human and animals, for food, territory, and mate; a carnivorous creation in which (as she wrote in a Brussels essay), 'Nature is an inexplicable problem, it exists on a principle of destruction'. Ellen's tadpole-reminiscence is free of the gilding of 'days long long a...go', as she held the note in her book of sentimental songs. You feel it is a scene Ellen would hardly have had the intelligence to dream up.

Charlotte described Emily as a 'native and nursling of the moors': *nursling* has a peculiar resonance. For hers was a motherless life, and she homed to the mother-world, sensitive to its seasons and weathers, pondering the flora and fauna of heath and grasslands. In *Shirley*, Charlotte shows her heretical sister choosing to spend her Sabbath in outdoor communion with mother nature, rather than in church. Since Charlotte's tendency was always to smooth and conventionalize her sister's image, it is fair to assume that Emily's heathenism was radically outspoken. She ceased to attend church. Nature was sacramental. Even the common grass under her feet could seem radiant and inspirational, as in the exquisite imagist fragment:

> Only some spires of bright green grass
> Transparently in sunshine quivering

'Earth', her favourite word, was playground and burial mound, a refuge in both cases from inward strife. Home sickness sounds a clashing chord through her biography. The death of her mother when she was a child of 3 was reinforced, more terribly, when her two oldest sisters, Maria and Elizabeth, died in 1825, at the ages of 11 and 10. From the sadistic bullying of the Clergy Daughters' School at Cowan Bridge, Charlotte and Emily were whisked home. Though Emily as the 6-year-old baby of the school was petted and no doubt exempted from its worst rigours, she had seen abuse practised systematically upon the gentle and stoical eldest sister who stood to her as second mother. The universe turned to 'a mighty stranger'; man and his institutions became factories for the mass production of lies. At school at Roe Head in 1835, she went into steep decline, unable to eat or sleep. The trauma burst up with each exile. She stuck six months teaching at the Miss Patchett's school at Southowram in 1838 and nine months studying in Brussels in 1842. At Cowan Bridge she had been exposed to the cruelties of a Calvinist regime which mortified the body to save the soul of the young sinner. Emily turned her back on the powers-that-be and their God. Homing to kin and moorland, she turned a Swiftian contempt on the manners out there in 'civilization'.

In *Wuthering Heights*, Emily Brontë shows an orphaned world in which the mothers die in childbirth, and the moor is a sanctuary which covers for their loss, as heath and bilberry bushes clamber the churchyard walls to gather the grave of Catherine Linton (who dies in childbirth) back into nature. Juliet Barker sees the loss of the Brontë mother as 'a commonplace occurrence – much more commonplace than it is today – and therefore accepted more readily. In a more pious age, too, there was the comfort of knowing that she had gone to a better place...' (JB 111).

Mother-loss *cannot* be commonplace. We only have one each to lose. Nor do pious platitudes compensate for having the centre ripped out of your life. Charlotte and Anne were to undergo periods of doubt in the Christian God. Emily and Branwell viewed him with Byronic contempt for his execrable logic and malignity.

Cowan Bridge, Juliet Barker goes on, was 'no worse, and in some respects more lenient' than comparable regimes (JB, 124). Charlotte and Emily had no vantage-point from which to compare prospectuses or statistics. To them, the place was death.

The proprietor, the Reverend William Carus Wilson, would count today amongst child-abusers. He cloaked in surplice and cassock a fetishistic interest in dying children. It belonged to an evangelical tradition going back to the nonconformist adoption of the *ars moriendi* tradition, in collections of seventeenth-century pious deathbeds, such as the saintly children described by the Baptist Henry Jessey in his *A Looking-Glass for Children* (1673). Dying girls were especially favoured. Jessey would sit at a deathbed taking shorthand notes of the dying child's utterances. Carus Wilson used this tradition to father horrors on the child-readers of his demented stories and poems, in which he feasted his necrophiliac ardour in a series of anthologies, *The Children's Friend*. 'Awful Instance of Sudden Death' in 1824 included the whacking of a lad by the sail of a windmill 'behind the right ear', killing him outright. The blade knocked him straight down to hell. A ghoulish finger seems to wag out of the text at the eyes of the reading children: 'Dear Reader, are you ready to meet the Judge?...escape for thy life, lest thou be consumed.' In Volume III of 1826, Christ's little ones are treated to 'The History of the Plague in London', decorated with imagination-enhancing pictures of corpse carts. 'Sunday Bathing' finds Wilson in ecstasies over God's peremptory drowning of two lads for Sabbath swimming. In 'Memoir of Mary S', he waxes orgiastic over the exemplary death of a 'very pleasing young girl, who had been for some months in a decline': he had been invited to visit Mary not to instruct her but because 'he was sure it would give me pleasure'. It did. As she closed her eyes on the pillow, she 'had by her one of the numbers of *The Children's Friend*...'.[19]

Emily Brontë found every reason to distrust authorities who had the care and upbringing of the young. Wilson, admittedly, was extreme. So was Emily. She was an extremist who subjected all the givens of her society to thorough appraisal and overhaul; and was quick to quit 'the common path that others run'. Charlotte reported in 1848 that Emily was nourishing speculations which set her hair on end: 'ideas which strike my sense as much more daring and original than practical... in advance of mine.'[20] The Tory, Evangelical–Anglican eldest surviving daughter of the minister was cagey about repeating these shocking opinions. They certainly contained a leaven of misanthropy bordering on nihilism, if the last poetry she wrote, in the year of the European revolutions, 1848, is anything to go by:

> Why ask to know what date – what clime?
> There dwell our own humanity,
> Power-worshippers from earliest time,
> Foot-kissers of triumphant crime
> Crushers of helpless misery,
> Crushing down Justice, honouring Wrong...
>
> Shedders of blood, shedders of tears:
> Self-cursers avid of distress...

('Why ask to know')

The poem has been called 'paranoid': she would have called it truthful. The focus is less on butchery than on mass self-deception and hypocrisy. People don't want to know. Their avoidance of reality is pathological, and expresses itself in systematic lies any child could see through. Anyone exposing those lies could expect no mercy because she would be perceived as a threat to the fabric of 'civilization'. Scenting danger in the world beyond the Parsonage, Emily hid in the camouflage of feminine domesticity like a refugee or dissident in a safe house.

In 1846 Charlotte's prodigiously accidental find of Emily's secret poetry resulted in the publication of *Poems* by Currer, Ellis and Acton Bell, which sold all of two copies; in 1847 *Wuthering Heights* came out; in 1848 Emily died. Her 'colossal' promise was singled out by reviewers; other deplored the novel's cruelty and violence as shocking, inhuman, brutal... words failed them.

When Ellis Bell's sex was known, the great question became: how could a woman have written this powerful novel? A young woman too, unmarried and living out of the way. Charlotte took Emily's wraith into custody, depicting her as a 'nun'-like innocent and possessed genius. She revised Emily's poems with mellifluous banality, smoothing out harsh truth-tellings she found unbearable. Thirty years later, T. W. Reid would assure his readers that Emily did not consort with criminals, as her novel might suggest: 'Of harsh and brutal, or deliberate crime, she had no personal knowledge.' Still, the problem remained: 'From what unfathomed recesses of her intellect did this shy, nervous, untrained girl produce such characters?' In everything but years, Reid felt, Emily Brontë 'was a mere child'.[21] The author of *Wuthering Heights* was 28, not some callow 17 year old. What male author would have been denominated a 'boy' at that age?

Some people felt they had the answer. Alice Law, *afficionado* of Branwell, was convinced that *Wuthering Heights* has 'an unmistakable air of masculinity': 'The very character of this terrible talk should convince any thoughtful or closely observant reader that no woman's hand ever penned *Wuthering Heights*. Such, indeed, was the universal opinion of the Press when it first appeared.'[22] So much for logic. *How could a woman have written the novel?* becomes *A man must have written it*, which becomes *Branwell wrote it*. This legend has deep roots in hearsay. Its assumptions echo those which prompted Heger's revelation: *She should have been a man.*

To contemplate these biases is to become freshly alert to the discrepancy between the face of a person and its perceiver: a warning Emily Brontë's novel also transmits. The task of winnowing observation from bias tempts the biographer tacitly to skirt gaps in understanding, or to bridge them with informed hypotheses. But what if the entire terrain around the 'dirty dots' seems comprehensively dead to the eye?

In the case of Emily Brontë, it is as if history had left us with a photographic negative: a brightly reflective image which translates to a nearly dark print. Evaluating the evidence of M. Heger, John Greenwood, Ellen Nussey, and even – or especially – her sister Charlotte yields a sense of highly lit blankness. 'Stronger than a man, simpler than a child, her nature stood alone,' as Charlotte memorably blessed her sister in valediction.[23] But Emily never presented men as strong or children as simple: the reverse. So much that has been written about her seems to refer to a ghostly double of whom little can be said save that it signally fails to speak Emily's language.

When I looked for Emily Brontë in these sources, it was like coming repeatedly upon tokens of absence, a collection of mourning jewellery such as satisfied the Victorian fetish for mementos in an age before daguerreotypes became generally affordable. A Parsonage display case holds a pair of white mourning gloves, issued at Emily's funeral, white gloves being the customary colour for *unmarried* dead ladies. The dingy white gloves, inhabited by dummy hands, surmount necklets and bracelets made from plaited hair scissored from the corpses of Emily and Anne Brontë, and lovingly woven for wear on the wrists or round the necks of survivors. Emily's funeral card is also there, printed with her name, birth- and death-dates, and the wrong age, by 'Joseph Fox, Confectioner'. No doubt Fox supplied the 'Arvill cakes' for Emily's mourners – funeral biscuits flavoured with caraway and wrapped in black-bordered paper, topped with a biblical quotation.[24] The white gloves are peculiarly resonant, meant to denote a deceased virgin, the whiteness an emblem of purity, the *tabula rasa* on which man's hand has not written. In an age before married women could under common law own property, even their own children; when they were still 'covered' in law by husbands (*feme covert* was the technical term), Emily Brontë remained her own woman, with her own name, which she signed to her works with pride.

When Charlotte married, her husband claimed the right to censor her correspondence. Before marital 'happiness' stifled her candour, she issued Ellen Nussey with a cryptic warning concerning the married state: 'I think those married women who indiscriminately urge their acquaintance to marry – much to blame – Indeed – indeed Nell – it is a solemn and strange and perilous thing for a woman to become a wife.' Perhaps there is a note of sexual dismay. And she found all her time usurped, 'constantly called for and occupied'. But she is very happy. 'So happy.' Charlotte insists on that. In the winter of 1854, she told her long-term confidante that:

> Arthur has just been glancing over this note – He thinks I have written too freely.... Men don't seem to understand making letters a vehicle of communication.... Arthur says such letters as mine never ought to be kept – they are dangerous as lucifer matches – so

be sure to follow a recommendation he has just given 'fire them' – or 'there will be no more'. such is his resolve. I can't help laughing – this seems to me so funny. Arthur however says he is quite 'serious' and looks it, I assure you – he is bending over the desk with his eyes full of concern.[25]

Arthur is a presence hanging over the writer, his eyes tracking Charlotte's pen as it speeds across the page. His censoring words are incorporated into the text, quoted verbatim, while he breathes down the neck of the author of *Jane Eyre, Shirley,* and *Villette,* dictating terms on what she may and may not write. Charlotte is mediating in this letter, seeking to keep open her personal space whilst placating the husband she loves. Ellen and Arthur are mirthlessly assured that his indignation makes her 'laugh' and is 'funny'. Arthur is not laughing. Ellen is not laughing. The modern reader is not laughing. For Arthur had it in his power to mute his wife, and was earnestly exercising husbandly muscle. Privacy and autonomy were not part of the marriage contract.

Ellen, passionately faithful to *her* Charlotte, gave an equivocating pledge to burn the letters – and didn't.

Can we imagine Emily Brontë, to whom privacy was life itself, entering into a bond in which you wrote under tutelage, dictation, or sufferance – and said only what you were permitted to think? Victorians puzzled over how a single woman could have written *Wuthering Heights*: our question might properly be, how could its author *not* have been single?

I shall try to track Emily Brontë through books she read. She was an omnivorous reader, some of whose books remain for us to leaf through in the collection at the Parsonage Library. The works of Shakespeare, Milton, Scott, Shelley, Byron, and the English Romantics, with the Bible, are well known to have nourished her mind. But some of the less familiar books she owned suggest clues as to the direction her mind travelled, sometimes in her own markings on the pages. The Brontës, father and children, expressed a rudely irreverent attitude to authoritative texts by seizing the margins, blank pages, and covers as, in Patrick's case, an opportunity for expostulation of personal memorandum, and, by the children, as a pen or pencil equivalent of a 'scamper on the moors'. In a household where paper was scarce, Tocquot's *New and Easy Guide to the*

Pronunciation and Spelling of the French Language,[26] acquired by Charlotte in 1831, was just the place to jot a poetical vision in pencil, and for some other child, perhaps Emily or Anne, to print the names of 'Gondaline Gondoline' by a sketch of three dancing maidens. What better use for the inside front cover of Branwell's Latin New Testament than for laddish pencil sketches of warriors in combat with swords or staves beneath a tree, a prone man being attacked by a wolf nearby? A doodled leaf or shell embellishes the Acts of the Apostles. Over a flyleaf in Dr Butler's *Classical Geography,*[27] dancing legs twinkle from under a kilt, beside the legend 'Lordly pig'; and someone has covered the next blank page in calculations in pounds, shillings, and pence. A page at the end of this book, favoured for its uncolonized continents of beckoning blank pages, seethes with doodles, cartoon faces, sums, scribbles, and, at the bottom, in dark capitals:

SATURN

SATAN

SATURN

The perpetration of marginalia, defacing the book, vagrant from the text, was not, of course, peculiar to the Brontës. Coleridge's *Marginalia* are among the most valuable of his writings. A later owner of the Brontë copy of Allan's *Life of Scott,*[28] John Binns, crossed out words and whole pages which offended him by their political radicalism, shrieking 'Shocking', 'The author lies', 'Stuff!', and 'Eh?' in the margins.

The Brontë children often ignored the printed text when they filled the space around it with their own anarchic testament. They were not commentating on the linguistic world but scattering fragments from an alternative one alongside. These child-vivified volumes affect us with an endeared pang of immediacy. More deeply, it is as if the margins rose in revolt against the centre. The child, occupying the narrow space left free by the adult culture, improvises from the ongoing play of her or his own thought-world, dreaming awake as one does when doodling, in a medley of figures and physiognomies, flirty or harridan faces, whirling dervish dancers, leaves scattered from the tree of the imagination, haphazard leavings which are perpetuated as the residue of a private life.

The margin is private space; the text authorized public space. That distinction was familiar to the young Brontë mind: their 'Brontë small script' ambitiously commandeered the gravity of print, standardized their works as a self-licensing centre. But marginalia have all the one-off freshness of handwriting and sketch. As girl-children, marginalized in their society, they ran loose on that edge, which became revolutionary territory, with its own laws and freedoms; as northerners (probably with a vestigial Irish brogue on their tongues), they were to shake the cultural centre; as gentlefolk on the verge of poverty, they eked spare paper, compensating for cramped space by cultivating single-minded intensity. For women in the nineteenth century, the private sphere was also their proper sphere. Emily seized advantage of her disadvantages: biding at home, behind the demure-looking front of beating carpets and baking bread, she could develop her gift in immunity. Freed from the tyranny of the consensual, she took the liberty of those edged to one side, to 'be as God made her'.

In *Wuthering Heights*, Lockwood pokes through Catherine's books. He does exactly what we do in turning the leaves of Emily's books:

> It was a Testament, in lean type, and smelling dreadfully musty: a fly-leaf bore the inscription – 'Catherine Earnshaw, her book', and a date some quarter of a century back.
>
> I shut it, and took up another, and another, till I had examined all. Catherine's library was select, and its state of dilapidation proved it to have been well used, though not altogether for a legitimate purpose; scarcely one chapter had escaped a pen-and-ink commentary – at least, the appearance of one – covering every morsel of blank that the printer had left.
>
> Some were detached sentences; other parts took the form of a regular diary, scrawled in an unformed, childish hand. At the top of an extra page, quite a treasure probably when first lighted on, I was greatly amused to behold an excellent caricature of my friend Joseph, rudely yet powerfully sketched.
>
> An immediate interest kindled within me for the unknown Catherine, and I began, forthwith, to decypher her faded hieroglyphics.
>
> 'An awful Sunday!' ...   (*WH* 18)

The effect of the diary on the reading Lockwood and on

ourselves, reading over his shoulder, is haunting: the child's testament is vehemently authentic, discharging the smarting moment onto the page with the time-arresting impact exerted by Emily's and Anne's diary papers, with their thumbnail sketches and snatches of humdrum chat which skims passing moments' reality. Lockwood insists on the antiquity of the books Catherine has defaced. The fungi and mildews that colonize dead books inhabit the viscera of these tomes, for, to Lockwood's nose, the Testament smells 'dreadfully musty'. The malodour of the past informs these sacred texts, desecrated by the speeding hand of the youthful diarist. But this hand too is latterday, the date of acquisition 'some quarter of a century back'. However, its virulent cartoon of Joseph bridges the generations: he inhabits a perpetual here and now.

The transcript, when it comes, electrifies us with the timbre of a rawly childish voice, bursting out in protest: 'An awful Sunday!' The past is exposed as a clandestine space whose voices may still be heard chiding, ranting, bullying, defying, weeping. The novel scoops from oblivion a complex scene of family strife in the same room where Lockwood has barged into its sequel. The 'arch of the dresser' he had noted is now understood as a refuge. It frames a frail sanctuary for the children, behind an improvised screen rigged from pinafores, violated by Joseph as he yanks the sabbath-breakers out. The effect of these illegitimate jottings is to dismiss Lockwood, for the time being, to the margins of *Wuthering Heights*. The girl's private testament takes the centre and the official print of the book she vandalizes remains unread. The narrator recedes into a mere reader, a frame round a picture, so that we establish ourselves in a new (but bygone) present tense, recurring to the time when Catherine 'reached this book, and a pot of ink from a shelf, and pushed the house-door ajar to give me light, and I have got the time on with writing for twenty minutes' (*WH* 20). The novel constantly displaces and replaces narrators until they are frames within frames within frames – a potentially infinite series of recessions.

Later, we shall realize that the diary takes us back to the crisis which separated Catherine and Heathcliff from sharing the same bed: the beginning of the end. When Heathcliff, 'my companion', expresses impatience with her writing and suggests

35

a 'scamper on the moors', he is making this suggestion from within the boxbed he shares with Cathy. The second extract records Hindley's separation of the children, so that 'My head aches, till I cannot keep it on the pillow: and still I can't give over' (*WH* 20). Snuggling in together, Cathy would rest 'her darling head on the same pillow as she did when a child' (*WH* 290). The gap between the first and second parts of the diary represents the trauma which Catherine, translated to 'Mrs Linton' at the Grange, will recall as the pattern of all succeeding separations:

> I thought as I lay there with my head against that table leg, and my eyes dimly discerning the grey square of the window, that I was enclosed in the oak-panelled bed at home; and my heart ached with some great grief which, just waking, I could not recollect... and most strangely, the last seven years of my life grew a blank! I did not recall that they had been at all. I was a child; my father was just buried, and my misery arose from the separation that Hindley had ordered between me and Heathcliff – I was laid alone, for the first time... (*WH* 125)

Lockwood now inhabits the space of Catherine-and-Heathcliff; as fellow-readers, we have also got in. In a novel of displacements and substitutions, the reader's mind is also at once lured in and barred out. The diary, which whets our curiosity, balks it. Like the Brontë marginalia, it is a mere snatch from a blanked-out continuum of life. The voice strikes us with the sense of Catherine's youthful vigour, yet, returning to Lockwood's present, we are jarred by realization that the child is dead-and-gone. A sense of discovery is framed in a recurrent knowledge of irretrievable loss. But then Lockwood dreams her up again, arousing us to wonder and speculation. In this way, the reading experience recapitulates on the literary level the experiences at the heart of *Wuthering Heights*. Playing with time, the costive author offers scraps of salvage, framed glimpses, the echo of past in present, the read in the written, the writer in the reader. Flickering between teller and tale, dream and consciousness, action and reminiscence, the novel mesmerizes us by its play of margin against centre.

Lockwood falters from the pathless snowscape, with its treacherous anti-landmarks. Snow-scenes always fascinated

Emily Brontë as the radiant burial of the already buried, or the transformation of liquid to a crust covering itself:

> Then let us sit and watch the while
> The blue ice curdling on the steam.

('How still, how happy' (1838))

Here was a 20-year-old whose eyesight had dwelt on the transforming processes of the natural world, whose chemistry under extremes of cold turned water solid and milk-blue before your eyes.

The winter landscape was a theatre of cyclical reburial:

> Cold in the earth and the deep snow piled above thee,
> Far, far removed, cold in the dreary grave
>
> .   .   .   .
>
> Cold in the earth, and fifteen wild Decembers
> From those brown hills have melted into spring –
> Faithful indeed is the spirit that remembers
> After such years of change and suffering.

('R. Alcona to J. Brenzaida' (1845))

Emily was fond of dirge or requiem (here for one of her Gondal heroes, Julius Brenzaida) and put her heart into them. Valediction beckoned, and wanderers in exilic loss enthralled her imagination; Gondal separations and infidelities allowed her real traumas to convert to zestful recreations. There is a spring and liveliness in her winter verse, which speaks of a remedial capacity to amend her griefs in the telling:

> It was night, and on the mountains
> Fathoms deep the snow-drifts lay;
> Streams and waterfalls and fountains
> Down in darkness stole away.
>
> Long ago the hopeless peasant
> Left his sheep all buried there:
> Sheep that through the summer pleasant
> He had watched with fondest care.

In Emily's version of pastoral, death covers the landscape in white scintillation of burial: *Et in Arcadia ego*. A reader cannot help but imagine the refrigerated flock preserved below. Emily Brontë had that 'wit' which is, in Schlegel's memorable phrase, 'an explosion of the compound spirit'. There is nothing of the sepulchral mooning of the sub-Tennysonian dolours that fed the imaginations of a generation of Victorian poets. The sarcophagal mentality was far from her thoughts, which bound through an outdoor universe which is a force field of mental energy.

Emily's *Winterreise* was made with a relentless jauntiness of step, by a trespasser over perilous landscape:

> Now no more a cheerful ranger
> Following pathways known of yore,
> Sad he stood a wildered stranger
> On his own unbounded moor.

Here the Emily-persona is in the position of Lockwood scanning for sign posts on the wasteland of the moor. Snowdrifts like quicksands challenged the poet's eye to divine a route across the barren, daring the reader to follow. In 'To a Wreath of Snow' (1837) the speaker aspires to cold altitude as a home-world of 'cloudy skies and mountains bare':

> The dearest to a mountaineer,
> Who, all life long has loved the snow
> That crowned her native summits drear
> Better than greenest plains below.

The woman who 'should have been a man' shrugged off feminine acculturation like a foolish garment fabricated for others, and casually claimed for herself the status of poet, pioneer, explorer, mountaineer, philosopher, musician, author.

2

'The Well-Spring of Other Minds': What Emily Knew

'Neither Emily nor Anne was learned,' wrote Charlotte Brontë in her 'Biographical Notice of Ellis and Acton Bell':

> they had no thought of filling their pitchers at the well-spring of other minds; they always wrote from the impulses of nature, the dictates of intuition, and from such stores of observation as their limited experience had enabled them to amass. (*WH* 366)

Charlotte's propaganda campaign, expressly mounted 'to wipe the dust off their gravestones, and leave their dear names free from soil', was a clean-up operation which manœuvred to present her anomalous sisters to the public in an immaculate state. But why should Charlotte have been so eager to assure readers that the women were unlearned? Ashamed of the brutal candour of *The Tenant of Wildfell Hall*, a book which she wished had never been written, and the amorality of *Wuthering Heights*, Charlotte made the excuse that her sisters were innocents, who did not know what they were doing. To claim for them a kind of intellectual virginity, she had to pretend that they were unacquainted with the world. I want to establish the nature and scope of Emily Brontë's intellectual interests, in particular what she brought home with her from Brussels.

She might have been braced and fortified by the potted life history of Beethoven, her favourite composer, as set out in the eight-volume anthology of sheet music she acquired in 1844, within two years of her return from Brussels:

> BEETHOVEN, *Ludwig van*, born at Bonn, December 17, 1774. His first master was Neefe; afterwards he took instruction from Haydn.... He finally settled at Vienna, where he died on the 26th of March

1827.... His life was *devoid of incident,* for during the greater portion of it he suffered under the infliction of deafness, which *confined him to one country, and deterred him from entry into society; but* he was indisputably the musical glory of the present century.[1]

Such a *curriculum vitae* must have been tonic to any aspiring geniuses whose lives had been constricted – lacking, that is, in the privileged cosmopolitan experience supposed to equip a man for greatness. A woman, confined to the 'perfectly secluded life' (Charlotte's description of Emily's world) in the company of a cottage piano, might find Beethoven's confinement bracing.

But Emily Brontë *had* been abroad. With her visit to Brussels, she became a European. Brussels put her in touch with the modern thought, poetry, and music of the Continent, which she can be traced consolidating on her return. When Emily and Charlotte left Brussels for their aunt's funeral in November 1842, Heger wrote to Mr Brontë regretting their departure and praising their remarkable progress as the fruits of 'love of work' and 'diligence'. He pointed out that Emily was to have taken piano lessons *'du meilleur professeur que nous avons en Belgique* (the best teacher we have in Belgium) (*L.* 298–300). Heger was honour-bound to consider his own brother-in-law, M. Chapelle, a teacher at the Royal Conservatory, a highly superior article; but Heger would never have engaged him to teach Emily had he not recognized Emily's aptitude and dedication.

Ellen Nussey went into ecstasies over the 'precision and brilliancy' of Emily's piano-playing (*L.* 599). These transports might be forgiven any excess, coming as they did from the renderer of 'Put me in my Little Bed' and other ditties. To such a novice, Emily may well have seemed a maestro. But was Ellen's praise excessive? Heger's recognition of her powers cannot possibly be attributed to ecstasy. Her name *Brontë* is the Greek word for 'thunder', and he had been treated to thunderbolts of rudeness in the shape of Emily's essays.

In July, he set his two English pupils the polite exercise of writing a French invitation and refusal. Emily chose an invitation to a musical soirée. A pupil invites her (female) music teacher, who declines with a decided negative, comforting herself for her absence by the thought that 'I will not undergo the mortification of witnessing the poor results of my work with you', and advising the pupil, for her own sake, 'to choose a time when everyone is occupied with something other than music, for I fear that your performance will be a little too remarkable' (*BE* 140–3). Dismissive of music-botching young females, who play as a party-trick, Emily indicates to Heger that music is too serious a matter to be trifled with.

Emily's connection with the *Conservatoire* reminds us that, during her nine-month visit of 1842, she would have had a chance to hear Beethoven's Second, Third, and Seventh Symphonies, the 'Egmont' and 'Leonora' overtures, and a Mendelssohn oratorio at a gala concert. The city was rich in chamber music and piano recitals. Berlioz visited to conduct his own *Symphonie Fantastique*.[2] We have no idea which, if any of these, she attended, but the gap between this and the calibre of the music available in Haworth was vast. On her return, she might have been treated to a vocal and instrumental concert in the church Sunday school, featuring Thomas Parker, the Haworth tenor, and Mrs Boocock from Halifax, with the orchestra of Haworth players led by Mr Hoffman, 'the celebrated...German violinist', said by the *Bradford Observer* to have 'astonished a numerous audience' by a cello-rendering of a piece called 'The Farmyard' (*JB* 408).

Emily was interested solely in playing, rather than in accompanying herself in singing: none of the vocal music in the new anthology shows any markings. Fine ladies were trained songsters, and might also have some arty showpieces up their sleeves. George Eliot, friend of the composer and virtuoso pianist, Franz Liszt, dwelt much on the difference between the trilling and tinkling of drawing-room music and the 'large rendering of noble music' which her character, Rosamond Vincy, catches from her teacher in *Middlemarch* (1871–2).[3] Klesmer in *Daniel Deronda* (1876), standing for European high culture, articulates the distinction:

> You have exercised your talents....from the drawing-room *stand-punkt*. My dear Fräulein, you must unlearn all that. You have not yet conceived what excellence is...You must know what you have to strive for, and then you must subdue your mind and body to unbroken discipline. Your *mind*, I say.[4]

In something of the same spirit Emily Brontë repudiated her Wheelwright pupils' reluctance to tackle the piano at playtime. Serious commitment to music on the part of a woman was deep in the European tradition. Women virtuosi were respected: Mozart had composed his piano concerto in E flat, K271, for the French virtuoso, Mademoiselle Jeunehomme (1777), and another (perhaps K456) for the renowned Maria Theresia Paradis. Clara Wieck, who married Schumann, was Emily's age, had given recitals from 1830, and became a composer of considerable power. Emily Brontë's skills could never have begun to compare with such virtuosi: but the achievement of women musicians in Europe was an empowering model. She returned to England with a vastly extended musical repertoire and a sense of the possibilities of music as a language.

Her purchase of *The Musical Library* in 1844 was a way of entering the German tradition more deeply. The anthology includes four volumes of vocal music, including Beethoven's setting of Goethe's 'Mignon' from *Wilhelm Meister* and Schubert *Lieder*. But her interest centred on the other four volumes of compositions or transcriptions for piano, a storehouse of demanding and fulfilling modern music. The preface to Volume IV Instrumental (March 1837) explains the collection's rationale: rebuking the fashion for 'frothy trash' whose aim was mere 'manual dexterity' and display of 'sleight-of-hand', *The Musical Library* has

> introduced, to a wide circle, compositions of a superior order, with which few, comparatively speaking, were acquainted...and has brought forward again composers of the highest merit....It has enabled thousands who never before had such an experience offered them, to form acquaintance with the great symphonies, quartets, &c, of Germany...[5]

A symphony in your sitting room...yourself a one-woman orchestra through whose two hands the spirit of Beethoven's Pastoral Symphony, 'Part of the Middle Movements of Beethoven's Seventh Symphony', the overture to *Fidelio* – Bach, Handel, Mozart, Haydn, Dussek, Gluck – might be transmitted: this must have kindled the spirit. Music had belonged to a cultured urban elite. *The Musical Library* promises to open out this closed circle democratically to 'thousands' who never had a chance of learning more than tinkling frivolity. The contents page of Volume III Instrumental is heavily marked by Emily Brontë's pencil. It shows us that she was studying and playing a six-page excerpt from Beethoven's Pastoral Symphony, No. 6, of 1808, starting with the first phrase, from which nearly all the first movement exfoliates:

Romanticism and the revolutionary classicism practised by Beethoven explored the link between the arts – music, art, sculpture, literature. Beethoven described the Pastoral as 'Recollections of country life', 'more the expression of feeling that tone-painting', opening vistas of countryside to the listener, with its celebrated evocations of bird calls (identified in his hand on the manuscript as 'nightingale, quail and cuckoo'), its brook, forest, peasant merry-making, F minor storm and 'thunder-basses', with 'raindrop-quavers'. As painting could be musical, and music painterly, literature could be both. The long extract in Emily's music book is marked out with a circle, along with another Beethoven piece, and music by Gluck, Handel, and Mehul. In Volume IV Instrumental, a selection from Beethoven's Fourth Symphony is marked, along with Dussek, Haydn, Handel, Geminiani, Mozart, and others.

Her markings show a characteristic aspiration to the symphonic, choosing works of technical challenge, which are spiritually searching and of some magnitude. In playing extracts from Beethoven's Fourth, she would be re-creating on the cottage piano in her father's study a sense of immense space, with the slow introduction of minor key darkness and its mysteriously measured tread. The practice current then (though today scorned by purists) of transcribing orchestral works for single instruments seems to me hauntingly appropriate to the symphonic compass of Emily Brontë's novel: a sense of cosmic reverberation confined in little space. The fragile cottage piano which Mr Brontë had bought in Halifax or Leeds for her and Anne in 1833 or 1834 must have flinched from the pounding Emily gave it when she returned from the superior one she had been playing in Brussels. Still, it had 5½ octaves and pedals. It is still there in the Parsonage today, and seems a puny enough instrument, with its mahogany casing and pleated silk screen hiding the strings. On those cheap keys, she internalized symphonic spaciousness in a private world. Ellen Nussey noted that Emily would never play if she thought people 'other than the family circle' were listening (*L.* 599). Inspecting her pre-Brussels sheet music, one has the sense of finicking, arduous labour (spidery fingerings crawl throughout one volume) and intellectual enquiry into the particularities of individual style. A set of variations by Latour on a theme in the manner of twenty-six composers from Dussek to Kramer bears heavy pencil markings.

Before I consider *Wuthering Heights* as a musician's novel, it is essential to recall that Emily Brontë was essentially a *lyric* poet, whose inspiration found expression in concise distillations of emotion. Music is a language, a sign-system with its own unfolding logic and laws; Emily Brontë thought musically. But her earlier work had not been symphonic in compass. Emily Brontë's lyric poetry shows from the first a musical ear attuned to phrasings and cadences of an expressive but restrained reverie:

> Fall, leaves, fall; die, flowers, away;
> Lengthen night and shorten day...
>
> ('Fall, leaves, fall' (1838))

Andante cantabile, the poet slows the first line to autumnal recessional, as stressed monosyllables balance around the caesura, dismissing with graceful irony a mortal summer. From the first, Emily times the lines of fragments like these with exquisite assurance: their music must have been running through her head day and night. The most haunting quality of her poetic voice is its personal, private quality, as if to live so abstruse and anchoritic a life had preserved for her a sanctuary of expression where central truths could be told with simple eloquence:

> O may I never lose the peace
> That lulls me gently now,
> Though time should change my youthful face,
> And years should shade my brow!
>
> True to myself, and true to all,
> May I be healthful still,
> And turn away from passion's call,
> And curb my own wild will.
>
> ('All day I've toiled' (1837))

44

Here, at 18 years old, she assents to the discipline of the quatrain, whose regular pace, measure, and rhyme answer to the 'peace' she guards and pledges. The music of this inner and personal voice was adapted to the Gondal world: sometimes taking music as its own theme. In 'For him who struck thy foreign string' (1838), her heroine hears the echo of the guitar as a 'magic tone' uniquely evoking the past:

> It is as if the glassy brook
> Should image still its willows fair,
> Though years ago the woodman's stroke
> Laid low in dust their gleaming hair.

Echo would haunt her short life's work: here the reverberation of the long-unplayed guitar string reinstates in the pool of memory phantasmal reflections of lost trees. A variant for 'gleaming hair' in the manuscript is 'Dryad-hair': spirits of place have long relinquished their green lustre in a violated sanctuary. Suddenly music's echo reroots their reflection. The image is powerful for readers of *Wuthering Heights* with its many mirrors of the living eyes of the dead Catherine.

Emily's lyric consciousness was from the first only deceptively naïve. Later she would learn to haunt her reader with a music whose beauty was severely abstract, as in her unforgettable address of 1841 to the caged bird:

> Give we the hills our equal prayer;
> Earth's breezy hills and heaven's blue sea;
> We ask for nothing further here
> But our own hearts and liberty.
>
> Ah! could my hand unlock its chain
> How gladly would I watch it soar,
> And ne'er regret and ne'er complain
> To see its shining eyes no more.
>
> But let me think that if to-day
> It pines in cold captivity,
> To-morrow both shall soar away,
> Eternally, entirely free.

> ('And like myself lone, wholly lone' (1841))

The ardently childlike note still resounds ('ne'er regret and ne'er complain'), lending the solidarity of grounded soul with caged bird a poignant authenticity; but the airborne extension

45

of thought haunts regions of spirit in which the 'shining eyes' are loosed into mystical or metaphysical freedom: *eternally, entirely free* vaults into abstraction. Echoic verbal music wreathes twinned, overlapping sounds in *eternal* and *entire*: death releases creaturely life into liberty boundless in duration and compass. This bonding of one word into its alliterative or assonantal partner became a principle of her verbal music, both in the poetry and the novel, with supple linkings of sound which calls to mind the Welsh *cynghannedd* tradition. But the effect is carefully underplayed: as a poet she learned from the first a light and tactful touch, pleasing to her musical ear.

This was just before Brussels. After Brussels, metrical virtuosity if anything increases:

Come, the wind may never again
Blow as now it blows for us;
And the stars may never again shine as now they shine;
Long before October returns,
Seas of blood will have parted us;
And you must crush the love in your heart, and I the love in mine!

('Come, the wind may never again' (1844))

The reckless rhythms of this Gondal poem are released with the bravura appearance of free verse: in fact metrical form is *regularly* irregular, moving with spirit between octosyllabics (lines 1, 2, 4, 5), hexameter (twelve syllables, line 3) and heptameter (fourteen syllables, line 6), a pattern relentlessly pursued through four dashing stanzas, which charge to completion in the final 'Me to strike for your life's blood, and you to strike for mine', the reciprocity of intimate friendship transformed to deadly give-and-take on the dynastic battlefield of civil war. Gondal remained a private world, with its inner dialogue and hidden history; yet, after Brussels, Emily Brontë's poetry and prose would develop a more formal public voice, able to extend its music to an anonymous world beyond the circle of self and life-guaranteeing sister-self in her confederate Anne. Courage to face outward was perhaps reinforced by a deeper understanding and mastery of musical language.

Musical language has the advantage over speech of remaining *essentially* cryptic, gesturing towards detailed nuance and shadings of emotion and expression, but remaining in the domain of abstraction. Transpiring in time, it may gesture to eternity. The classic sonata logic of exposition, development, and recapitulation unfolds in *Wuthering Heights*: the second part (in which the second Cathy returns to Earnshaw source) may be seen as all recapitulation. Dynamic colouring is expressive but nuanced. The text perpetually modulates between moods which clash, balance, and dramatize the play of emotion.

To notate a 'score' of *Wuthering Heights*: it opens with the bedlam scherzo of Lockwood's introduction to the Heights, style swerving between sardonic irony to plain telling, which is able to tremble at any point into the passionate expressiveness of (say) Heathcliff at the window. The narrative, however, neither lingers nor elaborates. The forward drive of the story is carried by a brisk and brusque no-nonsense *allegro moderato* as the tale passes to Nelly Dean. Here, English and Scottish folk ballad is incorporated: terse, uncanny, elemental. In *Wuthering Heights*, the second subject (Cathy II and Hareton) precedes the first (Cathy I and Heathcliff), giving a suspenseful shock effect. There are distinct climaxes and anticlimaxes through the novel, which the music swells into *appassionata* episodes of stormy lyricism. The first comes in the sublime poetry of Chapter IX, with its threefold movement from Hindley's manic but coolly told abuse of his child, to Cathy's revelation of her marriage to Linton and her love for Heathcliff, who absconds, and the storm scene. Cathy's famous 'great speeches' have often been compared with Jacobean poetic drama, but also resemble aria in opera, earthed in recitative: ' "I've dreamed dreams..."; "He quite deserted..."; "What were the use of my creation..." '. The turbulent music of the ensuing storm is varied in the brilliant manic vocalizations of Joseph. Quietening of tone follows, building to a new crescendo in Chapters XII-XV (Cathy's delirium and the frenzied adieu of Cathy and Heathcliff). An infinitely supple emotional movement between levels of *piano* and *fortissimo*, *adagio* and *molto allegro*, represents the author's mastery of the novel's tonalities – its exquisitely rhythmic movement from one range of emotion to another, echo beyond echo. If the second half represents some loss of dynamic tension, that is because it is seeking to reconcile the issues initially raised, in a formally satisfying way. The finale refuses the grand concussive climax of some symphonies: sound is quietly composed into the silence of 'that quiet earth', like the unearthly ending of a later Beethoven sonata, Opus 111. Measured cadencing throughout the novel moves between the tersely laconic and a disciplined lyricism.

In the diary paper of 1834, Emily had flaunted her musical turpitude: 'Anne and I have not done our music lesson which consists of b major.' Ten years later, there had been a prodigious amendment.

Upon her return from Brussels, she was observed to be deep in a German book. Kneading dough with her hands, her mind was concentrated on the open book (*G.* p 159). Why German and not French? Emily's French was poorish, because she refused to surrender to the language so as to 'think' in it. She wrestled it into distorted form by subjecting its idiom and rhythms to the laws of English. German seems to have made the greater appeal, as it had done to Scott and de Quincey.

Scott, collector and re-creator of the Scots ballad, novelist, and translator of the famous *Lenore* and Goethe's *Götz von Berlichingen*, ran in Emily's bloodstream. In 1835, Patrick had purchased George Allan's *Life of Sir Walter Scott*. Here she read Scott's account of how he kindled to German, 'this newly discovered spring of literature' as a close relative 'of the Lowland Scottish', key to a Scottish literary renaissance. Perversely, Scott tackled this by the circuitous route of first learning 'Scottish and Anglo-Saxon dialects', and tracking across.[6] In this way, he carried Scottish dialect, as Emily Brontë would draw Yorkshire dialect, towards the European mainland of language and literature. The quest for mothering originals was a fixation of the age: Goethe's search for the *Urpflanze* (the original plant) and the philological hunt for the *Ursprache* (the original language) expressed the same retrospective and recapitulatory yearning. Such quests represent the homesickness so intrinsic to Romanticism – and to *Wuthering Heights*.

When Emily Brontë was in Belgium, the influence of German Romanticism was in full spate in the French-speaking countries. England, insular, lagged behind, and through the 1820s–1840s, de Quincey, Carlyle, and Emerson worked to popularize its avant-garde ideas: dualist and dynamic idealist philosophy (Schelling and Schlegel); emphasis on the infinity of the 'world within', the night-world and the 'love-death' (Novalis); the pathology of 'split personality' (G. H. Schubert), with its electrifying effect on Hoffmann; the distinction between conscious and unconscious minds; the concept of 'Romantic irony'; the recreation of folk poetry and the *Märchen*, or folktale, as significant literary forms. These concepts would confirm Emily Brontë's binary mental world, at the stressful conjunction of idealism and realism. She is, as I have said elsewhere, 'the *sole* major English novelist with a full understanding of a dialectical philosophy'.[7] In *Wuthering Heights*, she dramatizes the strife of opposites, each essential to the other (at the simplest level, Grange against Heights; pale Linton 'civilization' against dark Earnshaw 'wildness'; nature and nurture; dream and consciousness; living and dead). But she also demonstrates the mutual necessity of opposites: to pass from Heathcliff to Edgar Linton is to substitute 'bleak, hilly, coal county for a beautiful fertile valley' (*WH* 69) – yet without hills, no valleys; without coal and arable lands, no subsistence. Catherine requires *both*, not *either*, and this triple bond is the centre of the novel's tragedy. *Wuthering Heights* also recognizes the co-presence of opposites within one another: for instance, 'civilized' Isabella Linton's potential for savagery is balanced by Heathcliff's early tranquillity with Cathy. *Wuthering Heights* works rigorously with a complex dualist logic.

A woman with small French and less German could not have swooped down on these ideas in Brussels and returned to her native moors a fully-fledged dualist. Rather, she must have picked up on ideas which struck a chord with what she already knew, and could develop systematically for herself. Back in Haworth, she set herself to learning enough German to read the language in the original. No one knows how far she got. The Parsonage holds Anne's *Pocket Dictionary*, signed and dated 1843, and a volume of Schiller's *Collected Works*.[8] There is also Anne's *Deutsches Lesebuch*, 'German Reading Book', including pieces by Richter and Goethe ('Mignon' – again). The only resonant piece here is Herder's dialogue, *Nacht und Tag* 'Night and Day', with its preference for the night-world as the place of female dream and vision, as against the hectic male daylight world.[9] Emily's night-poems, 'How clear she shines' (1843) and 'Ah! why, because the dazzling sun' (1845), express affinity with night:

> O Stars and Dreams and Gentle Night;
> O Night and Stars return!
> And hide me from the hostile light
> That does not warm, but burn –

'Does anyone thank you for your arousal?' Herder's Night demands of self-proclaiming Day, before silencing him in her stillness.

Blackwood's Edinburgh Magazine, passed on by friends, was browsed by the Brontë family with deep attention. It was read aloud to their father, a duty which Emily seems to have taken over after Brussels. Through 1842 and 1843, *Blackwood's* published a complete verse translation by Bulwer Lytton of Schiller's *Poems and Ballads*, aiming 'to communicate the mind of one country to the study and emulation of another'.[10] In the November issue of 1842 she will have read Schiller's 'Cassandra', the sombre story of the 'Prophet-Maiden', with her vision of impending Trojan catastrophe: 'Where'er I turn – behind – before – | Dumb in my path – a Spectre stands!', with Madame de Staël's gloss (quoted from *De L'Allemagne*) on the poem's meaning as the tragic alienation of 'all who possess a superior intellect with an impassioned heart...the true genius...is a victim to itself'.[11] The poem figures the prophet-poet both as female and as pariah in her community, her truth unwelcome to the junketing crowds at the wedding feast of Helen and Paris. The role of female as misfit seer was a heroic role apt to Emily:

> Unjoyous in the joyful throng
>   The still Cassandra wander'd on!...
> Into the forest's deep recesses
>   The solemn Prophet-Maiden pass'd;
> And, scornful, from her loosed'd tresses,
>   The sacred fillet cast!

Emily Brontë's 'The Philosopher's Conclusion', written in 1845, is a dialogue between the 'Space-sweeping soul' of 'philosopher' and 'seer', the twin halves of her poet's self, fatally sundered, in that the philosopher (divided in threefold struggle) fails to grasp the seer's intuitions. Mired in self-division, the philosopher's Cassandra-like affliction can find relief only in 'this coward cry | To cease to think and cease to be'.

In Emily Brontë's poetry, the eternally questioning soul strikes repeatedly against the barrier of human limitation, 'An endless search, and always wrong'. In her late Gondal poem, 'Julian M. and A. G. Rochelle' (1845), the visionary seeking the infinite, 'Measuring the gulf...stoops and dares the final bound', only to encounter the check of mortality:

> Oh, dreadful is the check – intense the agony
> When the ear begins to hear and the eye begins to see;
> When the pulse begins to throb, the brain to think again;
> The soul to feel the flesh and the flesh to feel the chain!

The Faustian search for entrance into the 'other world' was a major theme of Byron's poetry, associated with transgressive incestuous passion of brother–sister lovers. In *Manfred*, the Byronic wanderer calls to the ghost of Astarte in words that echo into *Wuthering Heights*:

> Speak to me...
> Speak to me...
> Speak to me! though it be in wrath; – but say –
> I reck not what – but let me hear thee once –
> This once – once more![12]

Astarte is Manfred's double, 'like me in lineaments, her eyes, | her hair, her features, all' (II. ii) Like Heathcliff at the window of Catherine ('Oh do – *once* more – hear me *this* time' (*WH* 27)), he seeks forbidden knowledge in the grave of his other self. But whereas the phantom of Manfred's Astarte replies, with a prediction of his death, Heathcliff gets no answer. The scene had created a matrix of Romantic poetry, haunted especially by women poets. Felicia Hemans opens 'A Spirit's Return' with an epigram from *Manfred*: 'This is to be a mortal | And seek the things beyond mortality'. The speaker, a grieving woman, succeeds in calling up the dead:

> I sought that lighted eye, –
> From its intense and searching purity
> I drank in *soul*! – I questioned of the dead...
> And I was answered...[13]

Hemans cleanses all the sublimely sexy trespass from her Byronic source. Constrained by the limitations placed by her age on a *poetess* rather than a *poet*, she treats the tabooed search for the dead by extending the icon of forsaken and abandoned woman. Romantic revolt is replaced by a pathos of alienation. The discharge of self against the boundary of mortality, in quest of a lost soul, begets an explicit answer from the black mirror of the beyond: 'One full-fraught hour of Heaven, | To earthly passion's wild implorings given.' Emily Brontë, however, preserved a classic restraint. She undoubtedly knew the Hemans poem, which opens *Songs of the Affections*, given by Charlotte to Mercy Nussey in 1842; but her instinct is always to refuse to pretend to know the unknown. A spartan integrity binds her hand.

The classicizing strain in the German poetry she read endorsed such restraint. Goethe's lyrics (printed in *Blackwood's* in 1844) confirmed the striving soul in its limitation. Schiller's persona in 'The Greatness of Creation' roves the firmament in search of 'Creation's last boundary-stone', a hubris confounded in infinity: 'Thou sail'st in vain – Return!'. 'The Ideal and Actual Life', printed in the edition of February 1843, is a dialogue between the earthbound and the sky-aspiring that mirrors a constant dynamic in Emily Brontë's poetry. Unembarrassed to wear her philosophy (and its dilemmas) on her sleeve, she refused narcotic, religious, pious, or Byronic resolutions of contradictions that must stand 'till I forget | My present entity'.

In September 1843 a long review article, 'Frederick Schlegel', had introduced to the '*un*philosophic English reader' 'a short sketch of the philosophy of Frederick Schlegel':

> The Germans have a proverb: – '*Alles wäre gut wäre kein* ABER *dabei*' – 'Everything would be good were it not for an ABER – for a HOWEVER – for a BUT...' But Schlegel's part in it is a virtue – one of the greatest virtues – a conscientious anxiety never to state a general proposition in philosophy, without, at the same time, stating in what various ways the eternal truth comes to be limited and modified in practice. Great indeed, is the virtue of a Schlegian ABER.[14]

The dual and contradictory mind represented the eternal dialogue of a universe at creative strife with itself. The article, though verbose, was a pioneering introduction to English readers to a mainland of thought alien to the English tradition.

Emily Brontë identified herself as a philosopher in a time when a gifted amateur might still prefer a modest claim to be an original thinker but in a country where dogmatic 'common sense' reigned. Her new lines of speculation inspired Charlotte with a very English repulsion, for Emily's notion of Reason did not strike her as very sensible. To Charlotte, Emily seemed obscurantist; to Emily, Charlotte appeared obtuse:

> In some points I consider Ellis somewhat of a theorist: now and then he proposes ideas which strike my sense as much more daring and original than practical; his reason may be in advance of mine, but certainly it often travels a different road. I should say Ellis will not be seen in his full strength till he is seen as an essayist.[15]

What these 'daring and original' speculations were, Charlotte avoids confiding. They must have been unTory, unAnglican, unfeminine, antisocial, pro-animal... marching determinedly *off* the beaten track. Charlotte's reaction is a compound of tight-lipped irritation at her sister's wilfulness and admiration of the systematic and forceful way Emily could reason out her views, so as to nonplus you when you tried to 'state the obvious' in return. 'Theorist' is a complex word in this context, somewhat derogatory, expressing a mindset parochially English, which distrusted feet-off-the-ground abstractions and liked to congratulate itself on taking up a stand on the bedrock of empiricism. Charlotte wrote in 1850 that Emily repudiated all influence: 'to the influence of other intellects [her mind] was not amenable.'[16] But, like the rest of us, Emily Brontë did not invent the word order; she entered into the discourses of her culture, which, however, she subjected to the analysis of a formidable 'YES-BUT' mentality. Schlegel's ABER must have spoken volumes to her. 'Hahsomdiver...' objects Joseph in *Wuthering Heights*, 'hashi-ver...' (*WH* 308). Hareton and the second Cathy dispute the meaning of the word 'contrary', pulling it in two between them: 'Con-*trary*' (*WH* 307). If Emily determined to stick to the Gondal 'rascals', she equally stood by her contrary vision as a 'theorist'.

The essays written in Brussels, translated and edited in a beautiful volume by Sue Lonoff, offer many clues to the direction Emily's mind was taking. In Heger, she met a worthwhile antagonist, eulogized in an obituary as having 'a sort of intellectual magnetism, by virtue of which he entered the mind of a student' (*BE* p. xxvii). Emily's essays repel the magnet by bringing into its field a more powerful adverse force of her own, part cold mockery, part anti-French sentiment, part personal manifesto. Heger seems to have been in his own way as highly wrought as his two nerve-strung English pupils – which is saying a great deal. So passionately committed was he to teaching and literature that he would burst into tears at his pupils' barbarisms or inanities, shriek and sneer, and glow like an oil lamp as he recited some sublime passage of French literature. Charlotte giggled at him as 'an insane Tom-cat... a delirious Hyena' – but volcanic emotion by Brontë standards was neither meretricious nor objectionable. Charlotte began to love him for his warmth and to yield to his charisma. Emily did the opposite. He complained that the essays submitted by the sisters were off the point: in Charlotte's case, this was perhaps a case of exhibitionism, the desire to arouse and provoke, and partly an unconscious use of the *devoir* as a courier, to send him occult messages of desire. Starry-eyed Charlotte wooed by submission of arresting homework. Bull-headed Emily charged the enemy. The dominance of a charismatic personality is a particular danger to a fragile and defensive ego, which needs to feel in control. The obituary praise of his ability to 'get in to the mind of a student' would have seemed a sinister intrusion.

Emily's first-known essay is entitled 'The Cat', and delivers a threefold punch in the eye of the unsuspecting reader. She likes cats. They are so like human beings, Emily purrs calculatingly – more so than any other beast (aside from small discrepancies of whisker, fur, etc.). Some people compare the cat solely with 'the most wicked men' because of 'their excessive hypocrisy, cruelty, and ingratitude'. Maybe so. But 'I answer that if hypocrisy, cruelty and ingratitude are exclusively the domain of the wicked, that class comprises everyone'.

Hypocrisy is developed by education (it is called 'good manners') and the other two flourish of their own accord, and are the pride of 'civilization'.

Cats sleek round you to cadge meat. What else is so-called human 'politeness' – lacking which, we are expelled from society?

Now Emily sardonically introduces a 'delicate lady, who has murdered a half-dozen lapdogs through pure affection'. *Madame* miaous affectedly that cats gratuitously torture their prey and 'you cannot make that accusation against us'. What about

Madame's fox-hunting husband, who tears the fox from his hounds' jaws before it is dead, so as to hunt it again?

> You yourself avoid a bloody spectacle because it wounds your weak nerves. But I have seen you embrace your child in transports, when he came to show you a beautiful butterfly crushed between his cruel little fingers; and at that moment, I really wanted to have a cat, with the tail of a half-devoured rat hanging from its mouth, to present as the image, the true copy, of your angel. You could not refuse to kiss him... (*BE* 56–9)

The snarling satirist here performs the human equivalent of house-training animals: she pitches hypocrisy face-foremost into its own ordure. There is malignity in her bringing-together of *Madame*'s angelic, butterfly-crushing brat with the predatory cat, into the field of osculation. Emily's anger mauls human self-delusion, the 'culture' that forbids a too close acquaintance with reality.

Feline ingratitude is just another name for perspicacity, she goes on: they see us for what we are – the wreckers of the planet.

Imagine *Monsieur*'s state of mind when this bomb was lobbed at him. Bouncing off its possible source in a passage by Buffon, it incriminates its reader in a universal lie which underpins 'civilization': the orthodox distinction between the 'animal' and the 'human' species. The essay refuses the social endorsement of human vanity. The essay is sprung with irony – deadly and deadpan, for Emily was out not to please by fulfilling her assignment but to displease. Only by refusing the lies legitimized by the curriculum could one retain integrity at the 'palace of Instruction'. She rakes vindictive claws of mirthless wit down the cheeks of the reality-refusers, stigmatizing especially silken, oily *Madame*. The butterfly-crushing boy is a chip off the old block of his father, the fox-tormenter. Anne Brontë, in *Agnes Grey*, makes a similar alignment, of sadistic boy with hunting adult: 'But you shall see me fettle 'em off,' he vows in relation to a nestful of chicks. 'My word, but I *will* wallop 'em! See if I don't!' Tom's sporting uncle crows over this pathological behaviour as male 'spunk'.[17] Anne Brontë reads the vicious attitude to creaturely life as an aspect of patriarchy which licenses male aggression. Emily focuses more forensically on denial: the essay spits at the fox-hunter husband; it chews up and spits out *Madame*.

All signs point to *Wuthering Heights*. We are in the presence of the author who trashes polite codes as the dogs floor Lockwood; the symbolism of animal ferocity which reveals aggressive drives at the heart of all human life, along with the whole spectrum of class and culture. The civilized Lintons are subjected to this scrutiny, along with the rest. In Chapter VIII, Cathy, 'in a blaze', has slapped and thumped, pinched and shaken everyone in range – like a wildcat, one would think. But the author reverses the obvious application of cat-and-mouse imagery. It is the 'soft thing', the civilized Edgar Linton, who possesses the power to depart, 'as much as a cat possesses the power to leave a mouse half killed, or a bird half eaten' (*WH* 72). We snatch a glimpse of Cathy as half-destroyed prey hanging from jaws that want her so badly. Isabella Linton, the infantile young lady, gets short shrift: Heathcliff attests that 'no brutality disgusted her... that pitiful, slavish, mean-minded brach' (*WH* 151). What we see of Isabella, laughing his pain in the face, embracing his code of ethics, tends to verify Heathcliff's character reference. Isabella's 'moral teething' at Heathcliff's hands forces her underlying ferocity to the surface. 'The Cat' regarded the class of the wicked as 'comprising everyone'. The essay's lethal and forensic irony is so bare-faced and tonally blank that it has fooled some readers into taking it at bland face value. Swift had also found readers capable of believing the solution of the 'Irish problem' to be the culling, roasting, and eating of Irish babies.

Another Brussels essay, 'Filial Love', faces out the Christian God's inhumanity to sinful man: 'Why add our malediction to God's? (*BE* 156–9) and aligns the speaker with the clemency of mother earth as she did in her poem, 'I see around me tombstones grey':

> Sweet land of light! thy children fair
> Know nought akin to our despair
>
> . . . . . .
>
> Well, may they live in extasy
> Their long eternity of joy;
> At least we would not bring them down
> With us to weep, with us to groan.
> No – Earth would wish no other sphere
> To taste her cup of sufferings drear;

> She turns from Heaven a careless eye
> And only mourns that *we* must die!
>
> .   .   .   .   .
>
> Indeed, no dazzling land above
> Can cheat thee of thy children's love
>
> .   .   .   .   .
>
> We would not leave our native home
> For *any* world beyond the Tomb.
> No – rather on thy kindly breast
> Let us be laid in lasting rest;
> Or waken but to share with thee
> A mutual immortality.

This moving poem of affiliation to the mother-world was written the year before the Brussels journey. Standing on its logic, her essay 'Filial Love' slyly solicits *angels* and men to weep for the damned. But angels, as she shows in Cathy's memorable speech in *Wuthering Heights* ('Heaven did not seem to be my home...') are not permitted to weep: they are inoculated against the sufferings of mortals. Angels are scarcely angelic if (as the Bible states) they pitched out rebels to hell; and heaven is less than heavenly if it can enjoy itself despite the suffering of the entire creation. Emily's intelligence is of the analytic and interrogative kind that delights to detect the fault-lines in a creed or system of belief, and to lever this flaw into a fissure, as a pitfall to her reader.

Her 'Letter from One Brother to Another' explores the complexities of fratricidal alienation, a dominant theme in her novel. But it is in 'The Butterfly', written in August, that the reader encounters original thinking, which bears profoundly on a reading of *Wuthering Heights*. The essay is dualistic, moving from condemnation of the creation as a construct of evil (exemplified in the ugly caterpillar) to an opposite and apocalyptic vision of a renewed and vital universe (the butterfly). But the opening sequences are the most gripping and forcibly argued:

> The entire creation is equally meaningless. Behold those flies playing above the brook; the swallows and fish diminish their number every minute. These will become, in their turn, the prey of some tyrant of the air or water; and man for his amusement or his needs will kill their murderers. Nature is an inexplicable problem; it exists on a

principle of destruction. Every being must be the tireless instrument of death to others, or itself must cease to live...

...why was man created? He torments, he kills, he devours; he suffers, is devoured...there you have his whole story...

...At that moment the universe appeared to me a vast machine constructed only to produce evil.[18]

In the 1830s, Charles Darwin too was jotting in his notebook observations on the chain of carnage in which all species were 'netted together':

It is difficult to believe in the dreadful/but quiet/war of organic beings, going on in the peaceful woods, & smiling fields.[19]

Emily's speaker views the recycling of life as a factory system based on a chain of predation, with universal pain its by-product. How, her speaker wonders, could saints in God's heaven bear to be happy, riding above the insane Creation? The mood-reversal pivots on the crushing of the caterpillar in the flower, followed by the revelatory glimpse of a luminous butterfly fluttering in the trees, which carries the idea of organic process into an imagined other world, beyond this carnage. Melancholy turns to sanguinity, as the voice reverses its assessment: 'this globe is the embryo of a new heaven and a new earth', in which every pain God 'inflicts on his creatures, be they human or animal, rational or irrational' will be harvested as joy. The fell universe of pain, as suffered by humans and animals together, is a seed of the new heaven and the new earth. All creatures will be reborn, not just human beings.

Acclaimed with relief by some readers as a Christian and orthodox conclusion, this is just a new heresy, if you think it through. There will be dogs in heaven. Cats too. Trees and heather. Hers is a Green and animal beyond, welcoming all comers. God would have to face some tough questioning from Emily at the gates of heaven. In *Wuthering Heights*, Catherine as a child of earth can also conceive of 'that glorious world' in which 'I shall be incomparably beyond and above you all' (*WH* 160). Although this vision of transcendence owes vocabulary to the Book of Revelation, most readers would be loth to call it 'Christian'. The question of a blissful eternity, 'where life is boundless in its duration, and love in its sympathy, and joy in its fulness', is raised and suspended. To Nelly's puzzling over the salvation of 'wild wick slips' like Cathy, Lockwood primly vouchsafes no reply, as the query 'struck me as something heterodox' (*WH* 165). The 'Green' heresy which sees the regeneration of nature in the next world has been a heretical strain in dissident and occult Christianity since at least the seventeenth century. Jacob Bauthumley, who saw God 'in an ivy-leaf', was burned through the tongue for blasphemy; in 'The Book', Henry Vaughan saw the calfskin book in his hand, made from the forfeit lives of dead creatures, tenderly restored in heaven to source in living tree, calf and reed.[20] Vaughan's 'Green' vision would have moved Emily Brontë, with her insistence on the continuum of creaturely life in a common habitat; her undoing of the 'pillow' of civilization into the bird lives shed to fabricate it; her love of animals and her recidivist imagination of the church resolving into the living moor. She must have come independently to these conclusions, for I can find no record that she knew Vaughan. Emily saw the restoration of all creatures in heaven, or none at all. Heaven could not have been heaven without Keeper.

The Brussels experience was no university education: but it offered intellectual extension beyond her previous dreams. A brilliant woman, hungry for knowledge, could make a modest ration go a long way, by developing and varying upon its logic for herself. We may add one more signpost to *Wuthering Heights*, which Emily found in *Blackwood's* on her return to Haworth. In June 1842 the journal ran a superb article entitled 'Berkeley and Idealism'. What she discovered here could readily be synthesized with the Romantic Idealism which excited her self-enquiry. Berkeley, the author explains,

> holds that matter has no existence independently of mind – that mind, if entirely removed, would involve in its downfall the absolute annihilation of matter... The question is: supposing ourselves away or annihilated, would the external world continue to exist as heretofore – or would it vanish into nonentity?
> ... But *can* we suppose ourselves away or annihilated?
> ... although we conceive ourselves and all percipient beings annihilated, still the great universe of matter would maintain its place as firmly and as faithfully.[21]

Readers of Emily Brontë's novel and poetry will be haunted by these echoes of her obsessive questions and excessive claims. The mind-stretching concept of whether the world would exist at all without the perceiver founds itself on the question of what can be imagined. Berkeley, the Irish philosopher (1685–1753), made his aim the destruction of Locke's concept of external material reality. The being (*esse*) of material things is perception (*percipi*). The existence of all finite and material things is brought into doubt. Emily Brontë was being invited to look at the world: her pen, the moors, the sun and moon, her stockings and Aunt Branwell's pattens and ask, *Do you exist?*

Did the sun's reality depend on her being there to see it? If she died, would the sun perish? If the universe were annihilated, could Emily still exist?

Such idealist, subjectivist, and egotistical bundles of ideas, whether Irish or German, were generally anathema to English common sense. Dr Johnson famously gave the short answer to Berkeley by kicking the stone: if your foot smarts, and the stone moved, be sure the world exists.

Emily was not particularly satisfied with the riposte of Dr Johnson's boot. Her fascination with the non-common sense world of the idealists echoes in the world *annihilation* (literally, 'made nothing') in *Wuthering Heights*. The word recurs repeatedly in the Berkeley article, which goes on to claim that, though all existence is relative to perception, 'Non-existence itself is a phenomenon requiring a percipient' and 'no question … can, for a moment, be entertained which involves the supposition of our annihilation'. Death is literally unthinkable; therefore, it cannot be. 'We have nothing to wait for: eternity is even now within us, and time, with all its vexing troubles, is no more.'[22]

Why was Emily Brontë so tempted by these ideas? They must have seemed liberating, endorsing her one-off alienation from the tyranny of consensus. Indebted to nothing and no one, she could be afflicted by no loss, invincibly internalizing all being as an object of perception. Her weaknesses (the desire to hunker down, away from human eyes and tongues) could be glorified as heroic strength. She incorporated the obsession into a late and famous poem, 'No coward soul' (January 1846). God is 'within my breast'; other creeds are scorned as 'Vain … unutterably vain … worthless … froth'. The note of disdainful bravado is defensively present at the outset of this Idealist's manifesto:

No coward soul is mine
No trembler in the world's storm-troubled sphere
I see Heaven's glories shine
And Faith stands equal arming me from Fear

.   .   .   .

With wide-embracing love
Thy spirit animates eternal years
Pervades and broods above,
Changes, sustains, dissolves, creates and rears

Though Earth and moon were gone
And suns and universes ceased to be
And thou wert left alone
Every Existence would exist in thee

There is not room for Death
Nor atom that his might could render void
Since thou art Being and Breath
And what thou art may never be destroyed.

The thinking mind encloses the entire sum of the Creation –
'Earth, moon, suns, universes', to the ends of the infinity which
so seized and teased the mind of the child who had opened
Goldsmith's *Grammar of Classical Geography* at the age of perhaps
10. Some youngster's pencil has drawn a line in the Brontë copy
against the geographer's presentation of 'infinite or boundless
space', which the pupil is asked to imagine by following this
procedure: imagine a bound, and then beyond that another
bound, and then another...This is the volume where, in minute
print, Anne inked in Gondal place names in a list of places in the
'real' world, for instance, beneath 'Alexandria; a city in lower
Egypt', the discoverer has added 'Alexandia [sic], a kingdom in
Gaaldine'.

These additions have long been noted as the cheeky extension
of a childish game. Emily in adult life hung on to the 'Gondal
dream' far longer than Anne. If Berkeleyan idealism were right,
then the universe was a kind of mind-stuff. So too was Gondal. It
existed solely in the self; she bounded in her breast its universe. If
the creative mind conferred reality on the 'suns and universes',
who dared deny the credibility of Gondal, the sphere she had co-
founded and in which her mind lived? 'No coward soul' is a *credo*
on the part of the author of Gondal and (soon) of *Wuthering
Heights*. It exclaims the solipsistic omnipotence of the sublime

mind which can think all things into existence, and minimize the shock of loss ('not room for Death', 'render void'). Emily uses the poem to paper over the grave.

It is a boaster's poem. If this self-vaunting had been written by a man, we would surely have cringed at his breast-beating machismo: 'No coward soul is mine | No trembler...'. A woman coming out with such defiance was breath-takingly hubristic – Icarus' sister, not content with flying near the sun on her stolen wings, denies the sun's independent reality. Readers have applauded rapturously (though perhaps few of us understand it precisely), not least because such a power of self-assertion implies a feminist and subversive thrust. But gender in this solipsistic mind-world is simply not an issue. In a population of one, distinctions are immaterial.

The poem, however, represents a mood rather than a philosophical conclusion. Self-magnification Emily Brontë saw as a trap. Her sceptical and relativist intelligence subjected her self-glorifying tendency to corrective criticism. Her poems of 1844, 'To Imagination' and 'O thy bright eyes', show her mind mediating between 'Reason' and 'Fancy' (imagination). The 'hopeless...world without' singularly fails to answer the emotional imperatives of 'The world within', indeed jinxes them. If the faculty of Imagination brings release from the pressure of the outside world, intimating '*real* worlds as bright as thine' (emphasis added), 'To Imagination' sturdily balances its weight against total reliance on the creative imagination:

> I trust not to thy phantom bliss,
> Yet still in evening's quiet hour
> With never-failing thankfulness
> I welcome thee, benignant power,
> Sure solacer of human cares
> And brighter hope when hope despairs.

In this poem, carefully wrought in a regular metrical pattern of quatrain and couplet (a disciplined verse), a prudent persona limits its dreams of transcendence to off-duty hours.

'O thy bright eyes', written within a month, figures the inner strife of Reason and Imagination as a court-scene, in which 'Stern Reason' is prosecutor and the 'God of Visions' invoked as defence counsel. The speaker appreciates why her truancy from the public world should be taken to task. Rather than making grandiose claims for her powers, she entreats the Muse to argue for her:

> No, radiant angel, speak and say
> Why I did cast the world away;
>
> Why I have persevered to shun
> The common path that others run;
> And on a strange road journeyed on
> Heedless alike of Wealth and Power –
> Of Glory's wreath and Pleasure's flower.

Imagination is 'My slave, my comrade, and my King', a king she must resist all the more because he is the source of 'intimate delight – | My Darling Pain that wounds and sears', a potently erotic image which conveys the impassioned quality of the visionary experience. The poem searches into the deviancy of her solipsistic passion:

> am I wrong to worship where
> Faith cannot doubt, nor Hope despair
> Since my own soul can grant my prayer?
> Speak, God of Visions, speak for me,
> And tell why I have chosen thee!

Both these poems frankly confront the suspicion of transgressiveness in the secret self-pleasuring of the imaginary realm. They ask *am I wrong?*; grant that it is possible; and acknowledge the 'world without' as 'real', and the speaker's obligations to this reality as binding. The perceiving mind is boxed in, hugging the sources of its occult inspiration, little deceived as to the waywardness of its alienation. The twinned poems remind themselves that the 'phantom' power of the imagination must be mastered by will and reason, or you go mad.

'No coward soul' abolishes the boundary between self and universe by sucking all reality into the perceiving self. The extent of the Brontë hubris can be measured by placing the poem alongside Felicia Hemans's, 'Invocation' in *Records of Woman* (1828):

> Speak then, thou voice of God within,
>   Thou of the deep, low tone!
> Answer me, thro' life's restless din,
>   Where is the spirit flown? –
> And the voice answered – 'Be thou still!

> Enough to know is given;
> Clouds, winds, and stars *their* part fulfil,
> *Thine* is to trust in heaven.'

For Hemans the 'God within' is the biblical 'still, small voice' that spoke in the wilderness; the Holy Spirit left by Christ as 'Comforter'. Essentially an implant, transmitting a message of adjustment and humility, the voice speaks from beyond and must be honoured. In Emily Brontë's poem, the voice is a whirlwind of near-punctuationless disclaimers of the 'thousand creeds' to which Hemans's belongs (the Holy Ghost, the Comforter); Emily Brontë usurps its authority. The 'God within my Breast' is creator and sanctuary of life itself: a self-exalting wind that blows where it likes. The poem lets rip.

So too does Catherine Earnshaw in *Wuthering Heights*. Her sweeping imagination storms the barrier between her wilful dreams and the interests of others; seeks to dominate and administer the reality of the 'world without' in accordance with desire. Through Catherine Emily Brontë points up the Idealist's nightmare of ontological insecurity: the void and need under-lying the daredevil boasts of Romantic Imagination:

> I cannot express it, but surely you and every body have a notion that there is, or should be, an existence of yours beyond you? What were the use of my creation if I were entirely contained here? My great miseries in this world have been Heathcliff's miseries, and I watched and felt each from the beginning; my great thought in living is himself. If all else perished and *he* remained, I should still continue to be; and, if all else remained and he were annihilated, the Universe would turn to a mighty stranger. I should not seem a part of it. My love for Linton is like the foliage in the woods. Time will change it, I'm well aware, as winter changes the trees – my love for Heathcliff resembles the eternal rocks beneath – a source of little visible delight, but necessary. Nelly, I *am* Heathcliff – he's always, always in my mind, not as a pleasure, any more than I am always a pleasure to myself – but as my own being –   (*WH* 82)

This magnificent speech explores yet another variation on the Berkeleyan query whether, 'supposing ourselves away or annihilated, the external world would continue to exist...or vanish into nonentity'? But now another needy human being is asserted as the ground of identity: if Heathcliff were 'annihilated', the universe would turn to a mighty stranger. Cathy likens him unforgettably with 'the external rocks beneath' and Linton to 'the foliage in the woods', immutable but barren eternity against deciduous but mortal organic growth. She wants both; gets death. She wants union; is cloven. *Traum* becomes trauma.

'There is not room for Death', bragged the poet of 'No coward soul'. *Wuthering Heights* mocks this boast by making room for death, which her impassioned characters defy or deny, for *annihilation* is the unthinkable word. Cathy's speech is heroic and ironically prophetic: but the author inflects it with childlike rhythms, a wayward pettishness. These doubles are not only opposite in temperament, sex, and degree, but inhabit a fortress built on quicksand. Though the speech is towering, Cathy and Heathcliff are mutually dependent, symbiotic, reciprocally mother-and-child. Each is subject to landslide if the life-guaranteeing other shifts. These heroes are fatally weak, for all their strong language.

Ironically, Heathcliff has absconded just before this speech asserts their unity. Cathy is already parted from herself. When Catherine is dead, Heathcliff searches her out, digging down to her ('I saw her face again – it is hers yet' (*WH* 288)), in a version of Gothic, unable to credit the fact of *annihilation*. He seeks her spirit in a world where she belonged – 'I felt her by me – I could *almost* see her, and yet *I could not!*' (*WH* 290). There is a close coincidence between the language in which Emily Brontë figures her Imagination as a 'Darling Pain' and Heathcliff's 'pleasure and pain, in exquisite extremes... anguished, yet rapturous expression' (*WH* 331). Having covered the whole surface of the visible world with projections of Cathy's reflection, he either hallucinates or sees her haunting image. 'My soul's bliss kills my body, but does not satisfy itself' (*WH* 333). Heathcliff's pilgrimage in the second half of the book is a marathon in which he systematically 'annihilates' the perceived materiality of the universe, and reinstates a phantasmal Catherine as his reality. And if he sees her, she will be real – for him.

Berkeley had sought to conceive 'universal colourlessness, universal silence, universal impalpability, universal tasteless-ness...' and these Heathcliff gradually achieves. He stops seeing the agreed reality altogether ('I am surrounded by her image...' (*WH* 324)), throwing across the whole plane of perceived reality 'one universal idea', so that, for him, the world reverts to colourlessness, impalpability, and finally tastelessness, as he ceases eating the food of the malnourishing world, sustained by a devouring passion for the recalled being of Catherine. Emily Brontë turns the vision of 'the universe...[as] a mirror in which all creation is represented', as Madame de Staël glossed the German Romantic vision in *De L'Allemagne* (III. iii, ch. 10), into a universe of narcissistic mirrorings of a lost beloved.

We are never told what to make of this. Assuring Nelly that 'the dead are not annihilated', he is experienced as 'fiend', 'madman', cannibal, demon, monster. 'He's a human being,' admonishes Nelly. 'He's not a human being,' retorts Isabella. The reader, simultaneously gripped by and set back from the literary experience, notes that, when Cathy and Heathcliff have finished their *Totentanz*, the world is still there. Suns and universes have not ceased to be – as far as we can see. Heathcliff, Cathy, and Linton are buried in one equation, but how to work it out we do not know. All realities (even relative realities), the Berkeley article had tantalizingly insisted, stand relative to the perceiver:

> There is a world as it exists in relation to us: true. And there is the same world as it exists *in itself*, in relation to us: true also. But the world as it exists in relation to us, is just *one* relation in which the world exists in relation to us; and the world as it exists in itself and in non-relation to us, is just *another* relation in which the world exists in relation to us.[23]

The narrative technique which Emily Brontë adapts to this vertiginously unstable system of perspectives founds itself in irony, a mode which was second nature to her, as the Brussels essays show. Romantic irony caustically unfixes all planes of perception in relation to one another: many witnesses articulate variant tales from discrepant angles. Nelly puts it bluntly: 'You'll judge as well as I can, all these things, or you'll think you will, and that's the same' (*WH* 183). The relativist novel takes the form of a dialogue, puzzling with blind fingers the contours of the imponderable.

The world of spectres and *revenants* is conjured into the reader's imagination and suspended there. Of Schiller, *Blackwood's* wrote in 1844, 'even when the poet represents the supernatural as the faith only of others, he must still, in order to do this effectively, awaken some degree of superstitious feeling in ourselves'.[24] *Wuthering Heights* cannily generates in the reader a mesmerized shiver, taking the theme of the demonic double from Hogg, Schiller, Byron, and Hoffmann, whose story, *The Devil's Elixirs*, may have been a source of Emily Brontë's novel, but bodying it forth into a vision of needy children who, bereft of bondings, cannot accept the bounds of self or the limitations of the finite. Because this psychological dimension is realized with such empathy, the realistic context so solidly built and the narrative voice so matter of fact, a sense of something 'beyond' affects the most sceptical of readers. In this sense, irony works subversively to license what it seems to discredit. We come away with the sense of someone 'at the window'.

The dynamic and elemental aspects of nature in the book also reinforce its equivocation with the supernatural. The novel's treatment of storm may be linked both to the experience of the 'sublime' and to 'science', in a polarity which is at the heart of the novel. Heathcliff represents for Catherine 'the eternal rocks beneath'. But bedrock can shift. This happened in Emily's experience, in the unpoetically titled 'Great Crow Hill Bog Burst' of September 1824. In a preamble to his poem on this event, *The Phenomenon*, Emily's father explained:

> During the time of a tremendous storm of thunder, lightning, and rain, a part of the moors in my chapelry sunk into two wide cavities.... From these cavities ran deep rivers, which ... formed a vast volume of mud and water...uprooting trees, damaging, or altogether overthrowing solid stone bridges, stopping mills, and occasionally overwhelming fields of corn, all along its course of ten or fifteen miles. Now, the grand FIRST CAUSE of this...is GOD.[25]

The second cause was, Patrick insisted (erroneously), earthquake, triggered by electric storm, and he preached a hellfire sermon defining the bogburst as an apocalyptic bolt aimed by the Almighty to just-miss Haworth, which he might strike tomorrow, should repentance fail to be forthcoming. 'God has unsheathed his sword, and brandished it over our heads'. He also wrote to the *Leeds Intelligencer* and the *Leeds Mercury* informing them of the 'earthquake' and the wrath to come. Seven-year-old Branwell, Emily aged 6, and Anne (4) were out on the moors when the storm hit, and narrowly missed being swept away in the seven-foot-high torrent of mud, peat, and water. Their father's poem derived the event from the Fall of Man and linked it with the approaching End of the World:

> But see! the solid ground, like ocean driven,
> With mighty force by the four winds of heaven,
> In strange commotion rolls its earthy tide –
> Whilst the riven mountain from its rugged side,
> A muddy torrent issues, dark and deep,
> That foaming, thunders down the trembling steep![26]

Patrick's old-fashioned Augustan couplets, via Thomson and Pope out of Milton, are a world away from Emily Brontë's elated greeting of the unleashed forces in the natural and human worlds. But her experiences of phobia were akin.

Patrick's phobias were several, and sensational. His terror of fire stemmed from a blaze in the kiln room at home in Ireland and the firing of the thatch of his parents' house in the 1798 rebellion: this phobia caused him to taboo inflammable curtains and draperies in his household. Another phobia was triggered by the Luddite riots in Dewsbury in 1812: he slept with loaded pistols in the house overnight through his life, and discharged a warning bullet out of the window at the same time each morning, aiming at the church tower. The pistols came down to breakfast with him, still charged. Phobic about sore throats, he engulfed his neck and chin in a high collar to deter draughts or germs, commending squill as an antidote to this scourge in the margin of his medical manual. Phobia was normalized in the Brontë household. Emily's phobia was of *people*, rather than attackers, natural forces, or acts of God. Terrified by the human race, she ran for her life to her lair, where literally nothing frightened her.

What Patrick interpreted as God's moral retribution, Emily exulted in by focusing it as the sublime. The Parsonage library holds an 1827 edition of Burke's *Inquiry into the Sublime and the Beautiful* (1756). This seminal precursor of Romanticism offers insight into the conversion of experiences of horror into excitement in art:

> Whatever is fitted in any sort to excite the ideas of pain and danger; that is to say, whatever is in any sort terrible, or is conversant about terrible objects, or operates in a manner analogous to terror, is a source of the *sublime*; i.e., it is productive of the strongest emotion which the mind is capable of feeling....at certain distances, and with certain modifications, [danger or pain] may be, and they are delightful.[27]

Charlotte said we breathed lightning when we read *Wuthering Heights*, and talked about Emily as a force of nature. But Emily's was essentially an analytic mind, which meticulously crafted and planned the novel's intricate structure, from which C. P. Sanger was famously able to construct a precise genealogical table, with dates.[28] Emily was no force of nature: that was her material. Horror becomes delight under her hand.

Wuthering Heights as a 'sublime' text bears comparison with the scenes of Lear on the heath and Prometheus on the mountain-top, ranging humanity against the dwarfing magnitude of nature, cosmos, heaven and hell. What would be catastrophic, exciting dread in life, at a distance (says Burke), and as suffered on our behalf by fictional beings, becomes a source of curiosity and pleasure. Emily's novel focused her sense of participation in nature's seismic and destructive manifestations by the complex distancing technique of her narrative method. The reader's mind is suspended in astonished fascination (the literary – and safe – version of horror) as, with artistic cunning, the author associates her characters with the elemental in nature.

And the elemental is perceived as dualistic: the point at which the Burkean 'sublime', German Romantic philosophy, and contemporary science meet.

Catherine first expresses the concept of a dualistic universe, whose inhabitants belong to two opposed but complementary forms of spiritual chemistry. 'Whatever our souls are made of,' she says of Heathcliff, 'his and mine are the same, and Linton's is as different as a moonbeam from lightning, or frost from fire' (*WH* 80). For her adversary, Joseph, there are also two conflicting kinds of humans, the 'chozzen' and 'th'rubbidge' (*WH* 85). Swathes of nature symbolism reinforce the assimilation of the impassioned natures of Catherine and Heathcliff to the dangerous life-forces which burn at the centre of creation, combining both creativity and destruction in equal measure. If Catherine's and Heathcliff's souls are identified with lightning, fire, the furore of high wind, dynamite, Catherine the oak in Linton's shallow soil (*WH* 153), those 'bare masses of earth' which magnetize the second Cathy, we are enthralled and electrified by this discharge of energy. But we would not *be* them for the world. Terror and passion are sublime – on the page.

In this respect, *Wuthering Heights* precisely fulfils Burke's definition of the sublime, including his memorable anatomy of the psychology of monomania, which has much to say about Heathcliff: 'When men have suffered their imaginations to be long affected with any idea, it so wholly engrosses them as to shut out by degrees almost every other, and to break down every partition of the mind which would confine it.' (*WH* 35). We kindle at the reading experience of such overwhelming, unqualified passion. But what are we excited about? And how far are these elemental manifestations of Catherine and Heathcliff signs of infantile *damage*? The novel's realism suggests that the volcanic energies released are signs of trauma. Stormy and combustible when hurt, separated, or brutalized, the Heights children are at peace when left alone. Together, they are lambs, not lions. The image of Cathy laying her 'darling head' on the pillow with Heathcliff when a child is peaceful; they never quarrel, for 'When would you catch me wishing to have what Cathy wanted?' (*WH* 46). His interest is her interest – except when that excludes himself. They share an ego, but Hindley loosens the bond by degrading Heathcliff, and Cathy splits it by responding to Linton. So human thunderbolts are discharged by pain and need, and not for the hell of it. The novel asks us not to glamorize violence, at the same time as it revels in the sublimity of storm conditions prevailing among its people.

Charlotte Brontë had nourished a fervid juvenile passion for the paintings of John Martin, with his apocalyptic scenes of Babylon, Nineveh, Pompeii at their hour of destruction: cosmic visions of pyrotechnic acts of God, lurid and grandiose. The family owned at least four of Martin's engravings of the 1820s, *Belshazzar's Feast, Joshua Arresting the Sun, The Deluge, The Passage of the Red Sea*. Vast vistas of palaces blitzed dominated Charlotte's imagination. Her notion of the sublime is exemplified in descriptions such as this from her juvenilia: 'All beneath them were liquid mountains tossed to and fro' with horrible confusion, roaring and raging with a tremendous noise, and crowned with the waves of foam. All above them was a mighty firmament in one part covered with black clouds from which darted huge and terrible sheets of lightning...'.[29] This prodigious thirteen-and-a-half-year-old has read Milton and Byron, pored over Martin prints, and been aroused by a universe of grand effects – and adjectives. Confusion is 'horrible', noise 'tremendous', the firmament 'mighty', and sheets of lightning 'huge and terrible'. In other words sublimity implodes at every point in tautology. Emily Brontë's vision of the sublime is essentially noun- and verb-founded, attaining its effects through unadorned brevity and restraint. She too had read Milton, homing to the thrust and drive of his language. But her interest in *Sturm und Drang* had also, I would suggest, a matter-of-fact and scientific basis.

Patrick Brontë owned a copy of Humphrey Davy's *Elements of Chemical Philosophy* (1812),[30] which introduced to amateurs the concept of chemical processes and the categorization of chemical elements according to groups or families. *Wuthering Heights*, even more than *Jane Eyre*, is founded on the concept of natural sympathies and antipathies, which Romanticism had popularized but, additionally, modern science was claiming as the ground of all being and transformation. Davy's career (1778–1829) had developed from his work on electricity and chemical experiments; he was a friend of Scott. In *Elements of Chemical Philosophy* he suggested home experiments and observations for readers to demonstrate to themselves, for example, the eternal transformation of substances, which he instanced in the decay of 'leaves and branches of a fallen tree exposed to the atmosphere, and the rapid combustion of wood in our fires'. Both these are 'chemical operations' applied to organic forms. Matter of 'biology' becomes matter of 'chemistry'. For Davy, all processes depend on natural 'attraction' and 'repulsion' of particles:

> Sugar dissolves in water, alkalies unite with acids, metals dissolve in acids. Is not this, says Newton, on account of an attraction between their particles? Copper dissolved in aquafortis is thrown down by iron. Is not this because the particles of the iron have a stronger attraction for the particles of the acid, than those of copper: and do not different bodies attract each other with different degrees of force?

He emphasized Germany as 'the great school of practical chemistry', where Beccher 'formed the bold idea of explaining the whole system of the earth by the mutual agency and changes of a few elements'. The chapter 'On chemical Attraction' discusses the 'chemical *attraction* or affinity' of elements. Oil and water 'refuse to act upon each other, and separate', incapable of combination. Different bodies unite with different degrees of force 'and hence, one body is capable of separating others, from certain of their combinations... This has been called *double affinity,* or *complex attraction.*'[31] He continues with discussion 'Of Electrical Attraction and Repulsion', discussing the polarity of electrical positive and negative poles.

All this resonates in a reading of *Wuthering Heights.* Gondal had teemed with factions and families: *Wuthering Heights* selects a clinically concise number of elements (the poles of Earnshaw and Linton) and relates them through a systematic logic of bondings, compounds, and disaffinities, studying the interaction of these compounds in the second generation. Chemical processes are used as a way of displaying the contents and transformations of the psyche. The author works out a particulate system of affinities and repulsions, with predetermined inclination to unite or separate. Catherine's sense of the 'impracticability' of separating herself and Heathcliff is based on their mental chemistry. Being a compound made of one another's mind-elements, they literally *cannot* be separated: 'He's more myself than I am.' It cannot be done. In *Wuthering Heights,* all symbolism tends to the substantial. Heathcliff, 'hard as whinstone' (*WH* 33), 'an arid wilderness of furze and whinstone' (*WH* 102), seems to have mineral affinity not only with Catherine but with their place of belonging, 'the eternal rocks beneath'. And Cathy's genuine attempt to mate with Linton cannot succeed because their attraction is cancelled by the human equivalent of Davy's 'double affinity, complex chemical affinity', in which 'one body is capable of separating others, from certain of their combinations'. Cathy's bond with Linton is a loose combination, undone by the return of her primary affinity. Yet, as a genuine combination, based on mutual attraction, it bears viable issue in the second generation, just as Hindley's marriage to Frances does. In this second generation, Emily Brontë enacts a series of chemical transformations, so schematic that one might set it out like chemical equations:

HINDLEY + FRANCES EARNSHAW (attraction) = HARETON EARNSHAW (attraction)⎫
EDGAR + CATHERINE LINTON (attraction) = CATHERINE LINTON ⎬
HEATHCLIFF + ISABELLA (repulsion) = LINTON HEATHCLIFF ⎭ (repulsion)

Isabella's and Heathcliff's incompatibility issues in the abortive compound, Linton Heathcliff. 'Incompatible' is too weak a word.

Heathcliff views Isabella as 'a strange repulsive animal, a centipede from the Indies...which curiosity leads one to examine in spite of the aversion it raises' (*WH* 105). Ironically, Isabella degenerates into a mirror of Heathcliff's vengeful cruelty when bonded to him by marriage. The compound flies asunder in miscegenation and its offspring is no long viable. Linton Heathcliff compounds the most degenerate qualities of both parents. Contrasting him with Hareton, Heathcliff views the two as minerals with opposite qualities:

> there's this difference: one is gold put to the use of paving stones, and the other is tin polished to ape a service of silver – *Mine* has nothing valuable about it; yet I shall have the merit of making it go as far as such poor stuff can go. *His* had first rate qualities, and they are lost – (*WH* 219)

The trampled gold of Hareton's character, however, outlasts the base metal of Linton Heathcliff's compound of disaffinities, malleable to the force exerted by his feared father. In another mineral metaphor, Hareton's nature is 'tough as tempered steel' (*WH* 336). Emily Brontë structures the chemistry of second-generation matings in terms of the attraction of like to like, in the golden-haired Catherine to the underlying gold of Hareton, brought together by common qualities, the Earnshaw gene: 'their eyes are precisely similar, and they are those of Catherine Earnshaw' (*WH* 322). The author is able to suggest in her resolution of the novel an unpreventable mutual pull of sympathetic natures.

Process, therefore, is viewed as dictated by the innate qualities of elements, intractable to manipulation. Heathcliff's revenge 'plot' is symmetrical and logical, outwitting Hindley in the first generation. But the author's plot mocks Heathcliff's in the second, by making his success in bringing together Catherine and Hareton the means of his defeat. 'Hareton and I are friends now,' Cathy defies him (*WH* 320): they are compounded. The final end of Heathcliff's homing to his lost affinity can only be in the earth where the first Catherine lies.

Much is made of the chemistry of the grave, and its 'transformations', with the introduction of a macabre Gothic motif:

> 'were you not ashamed to disturb the dead? And if she had been

dissolved in earth, or worse, what would you have dreamt of then?'
[Nelly] said.

'Of dissolving with her, and being more happy still!... Do you
suppose I dread any change of that sort? I expected such a
transformation on raising the lid, but I'm better pleased that it
should not commence till I share it.' (*WH* 289)

The passage plays upon the key of D – *disturb, dead, dissolves,
dreamt, dissolving, dread* – keywords carrying both turbulence
and comfort. Go looking for the dead, says Nelly, and you will
find nothing more lively than the chemical process of
putrefaction. The passage cannily plays on two distinct meanings of *dissolve* – the repellent idea of 'dissolution', a change
which destroys the identity of the body by subjecting it to decay;
and the comforting idea of mutual becoming, which Heathcliff
seeks, on any terms. Catherine's 18-year-old corpse, putrefied,
would still, for Heathcliff, be Catherine. He means to become
one flesh with her waiting and preserved body, in the earth
where decomposition will become recomposition, a marriage so
complete that 'when Linton gets to us, he'll not know which is
which!' (*WH* 288). This macabre scenario imagines the double
grave as marriage-bed in which change (in a novel that dreads
change) is acceptable when it is a compounding of originals. I
have described elsewhere the Byronic brother–sister bond and
the inbreeding tribalism of the novel:[32] to view these genealogical
interactions in terms of the essentially *dynamic* binding of like to
like in the Romantic chemistry with which Emily was familiar
reinforces the systematic structure of the novel's reproductive
procedures.

The idea of *dissolving* also relates to the author's study of
mental processes and especially of the unconscious mind.
Catherine describes her experience of dreams in Chapter IX,
as agents of transformation:

I've dreamt in my life dreams that have stayed with me ever after,
and changed my ideas; they've gone through and through me, like
wine through water, and altered the colour of my mind   (*WH* 79)

'Sugar dissolves in water, alkalies with acids, metals dissolve in
acids,' Davy pointed out. The impressive metaphor generated
by Cathy repeats the experience narrated, in the mind of the
reader. *Wuthering Heights* has gone through and through the

minds of generations of readers, altering the colour of our minds. Do minds have colour? Are they susceptible of chemical change? We had not thought so before, perhaps, but the description seems to reach beyond analogy to express a fugitive experience of inner transformation which is felt as a suffusion by dream when we awaken, or the mind's mingling with the author's in the reading of a book. Heathcliff *dissolves* into Catherine; Catherine's dreams *dissolve* into her mind; our minds *dissolve* in, mingle with, and are wine-stained by *Wuthering Heights*. Even the suggestion of intoxication is felicitous.

The dream Catherine confides is intended as a way of explaining her 'secret' to Nelly, who doesn't want to know:

> I was only going to say that heaven did not seem to be my home, and I broke my heart with weeping to come back to earth; and the angels were so angry that they flung me out, into the middle of the heath on the top of *Wuthering Heights*, where I woke sobbing for joy   (*WH* 80)

This is a heretical play on a cluster of the novel's keywords which belong deep in the traditions of dissenting and Evangelical Christianity which Emily Brontë inherited and disowned. In the seventeenth century, the Puritan, Margaret Charlton, wrote in her covenant with God:

> Why should my heart be fixed where my home is not? Heaven is my home; God in Christ is all my happiness: and where my treasure is, there my heart should be.[33]

I choose this text not because Emily knew it (she probably didn't) but because it concisely arrays the biblically derived terms and phrases Christian women called upon to secure them in an uncertain world. To juxtapose these texts highlights Emily Brontë's revolutionary repositioning of the whereabouts of the sacred and of sanctuary. Both writers are playing in the key of H:

EMILY BRONTË: *heaven, home, heart, heath, Heights ... Heathcliff*
MARGARET CHARLTON: *heart, home, heaven, home, happiness, heart*

The cluster of words signifying spiritual affinity and allegiance involves for both women a search for belonging. But whereas the other-worldly piety of Margaret Charlton aspires constantly upwards towards a 'happiness' she conceives inaccessible on this earth, Catherine aspires downwards, like lightning, and is discharged to the earth which is her sole place of kinship.

Reversing the Christian and Miltonic valuation of Lucifer's fall, Emily Brontë's character smites God's totalitarian logic by bursting into tears in the bosom of a dictatorial 'happiness'; her sanctuary is (quite as paradoxically) the height of earth, in a joy so extreme that it expresses its homecoming in tears. This, of course, is meant as a parable: 'I've no more business to marry Edgar Linton than I have to be in heaven...' (WH 80) – a prediction fulfilled by her experience of separation from her likeness in Heathcliff.

As a work of Romantic rebellion, Wuthering Heights takes Promethean issue with human limitation, whilst earthing its thunder and lightning in substantial realism and bracing it in a system of attraction and repulsion, with its roots in science.

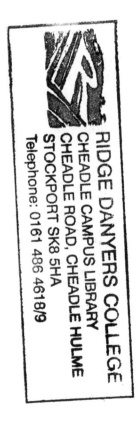

3

The House of Trauma: A Reading of *Wuthering Heights*

While *Wuthering Heights* is a book resisting interpretation, Wuthering Heights is a house barring out trespassers:

> A perfect misanthropist's Heaven – and Mr. Heathcliff and I are such a capital pair to divide the desolation between us. A capital fellow! He little imagined how my heart warmed towards him when I beheld his black eyes withdraw so suspiciously under their brows, as I rode up, and when his fingers sheltered themselves, with a jealous resolution, still further in his waistcoat, as I announced my name. (*WH* 1)

Language in both house and text signs a two-way contradiction. 'Walk in!' snarls Heathcliff. 'The "walk in" was uttered with closed teeth and expressed the sentiment, "Go to the Deuce!"'. Where 'come in' means 'clear off', perversity becomes a new norm. For 'Go to the Deuce!' is a come-on to Lockwood, who is disposed to take inhospitality as an incentive.

The building's paranoid architecture parallels the pathological defensiveness of the host, parodied by the loquacious Lockwood's pose as hermit. The narrator's gaucherie meets a pathology evinced in the 'withdraw[al]' of the host's dark eyes, his fingers that 'sheltered themselves, with a jealous resolution, still further in his waistcoat': Heathcliff seems to be coming apart from himself, but all the parts are in flight. The visitor, gaining entrance to the house, registers a vista of recession from outsiders: 'the kitchen is forced to retreat altogether' (*WH* 3). Black chairs 'lurk' in the background shade, while dogs 'haunt' recesses, and the careless reader may be forgiven for muddling chairs with dogs. The owner of this establishment, at once so substantial and so secretive, 'keeps his hand out of the way' and loves and hates 'under cover', as Lockwood speculates. Beyond the house, a panorama of weathered barrenness declares a landscape of universal need and exposure, 'a range of gaunt thorns all stretching their limbs one way, as if craving alms of the sun'. Spiritual beggary predominates. Deepset windows are 'defended' by 'large-jutting stones'.

House, territory, and owner represent a landscape of buried and inhering trauma: affliction so deep as to be repressed, unintelligible, untellable, beneath a mantle of domesticity. And the symptoms of trauma, including Heathcliff's manic control, suggest not primarily aggression (which is secondary) but plain *fear*. Heathcliff's instinct is to hide. He keeps himself to himself, on the alert for intrusion, reserved, surrounded by a pack of dogs, a matriarchy whose leader, 'the canine mother', slavers for a 'snatch' of the intruder's calves. The dogs act as an extension of Heathcliff's paranoia, exercising their 'jealous guardianship' over his premises. Associated from the first with 'fiends', 'spirits' (like Heathcliff's eyes), his proxies maintain ceaseless, insomniac vigil for him in his absence: a partnership – 'I and my dogs' (*WH* 6). Throughout, a solid normality bounds our attention and legitimizes spectral connotation by substantiating it in realism and plain description. Lockwood talks variously like a guide-book, chatty diarist, callow young gent on holiday, busybody. Through his careful noting of detail, the author concisely creates a room in the reader's imagination brimming with quotidian northern reality – a main room echoing with chatter and clatter of cooking vessels from the unseen kitchen beyond; roaring fire, 'vast oak dresser', guns, cannisters, green-painted chairs. Things feel solid. But the sense of an 'elsewhere', a 'beyond', is there from the outset. Lockwood lists the things he cannot see ('*no* signs of roasting... *nor* any glitter of copper saucepans...' (*WH* 3; emphasis added). The unseen is here presented for what it is, a perfectly normal aspect of everyday experience. We cannot be everywhere at once, and the novel forsakes the roving eye of omniscient narration to occupy the partial and hence occluded view of the eyewitness. Relativity of vision therefore begins to build, innocently, from the first pages, an aura of the invisible. Deep into the book, we shall begin, spellbound, to intuit the invisible as the centre.

The house, Lockwood assures us, 'would have been *nothing extraordinary*' in these parts, as the property of a northern farmer, aside from Heathcliff's anomalousness, for which Lockwood accounts by noting his host's dual social aspect: rough, swarthy gipsy, kempt 'gentleman'. The novel, then, opens in a non-welcome from a forbidding host. Lockwood's reaction to prohibition is, 'I shall go notwithstanding': a pertinacity he shares with all the novel's persons and readers. Where a secret is advertised, we rush to be in on it.

Emily Brontë hence creates in her reader, through the narrator, a drive towards comprehension, amounting to compulsion: when Lockwood, on his second visit in Chapter II, finds that Heathcliff has chained the gate, he vaults the hurdle and lambasts the door, murmuring to himself pettishly, 'I don't care – I will get in' (*WH* 7). And he does. Only to wish he hadn't. Bungling and blundering his way past the non-introduction he receives, Lockwood alights on Catherine's right name ('Mrs Heathcliff') by infelicitous mistake; misconstrues a heap of dead rabbits for a cushionful of lady's pet kittens; mistakes Catherine for Heathcliff's, then Hareton's wife, and is set on by all, concluding in a second attack by dogs. In this frenetic scherzo, the reader picks up the hem of the trauma, which is shared by all dwellers in the Wuthering household – Cathy speaks, if at all, 'more repellingly than Heathcliff'; Hareton, boorish and bearish, scowls 'as if there were some mortal feud unavenged between us' (*WH* 9). An identical blight seems distributed amongst them, the aftermath of prior affliction, recalled in Heathcliff's caustic allusions to his dead wife and Joseph's onslaught (to Cathy) on 'yer mother afore ye!'. These people are leftovers, the survivors of some catastrophe. But what?

In the third chapter, Lockwood homes in on the secret – with a vengeance. In he goes, guided by Zillah, to the disused chamber; deeper in, to the boxbed, where Lockwood (ironically) 'felt secure against the vigilance of Heathcliff, and everyone else'. Browsing old books, the narrator invades the private mind of a needy, naughty girl twenty-five years past, a Catherine of no fixed surname. But the books exact retribution. They invade his mind in dreams, which climax in the icy grip of the wraith of

Catherine Linton. Reading has given access to forbidden but incomprehensible knowledge, as he guiltily realizes when viewing Heathcliff's desolation as he in turn wrenches open the window in anguish and calls up the ghost of a girl Heathcliff cannot reclaim, but Lockwood (against his will) can. Reading has passed on the household trauma to the psyche of the alien reader.

We speak of 'getting into a book', of 'being deep in a book', but also of being 'lost in a book', yielding to the pressure of another mind, as one rarely does in life; and of being 'possessed by a book': 'reading [the name Catherine Linton] often over produced an impression which personified itself when I had no longer my imagination under control' (WH 26). Surely this is exactly what happens to readers when 'grasped' by the icy fingers of Wuthering Heights. Books haunt us. They beget images and impressions which can last our lives long, becoming part of our personal and communal life. But if Emily Brontë's novel remains 'in solution' with the reader's mind, there is never a sense that we have a 'solution' to it. Lockwood stands for us (though we distance ourselves from his follies) as a reader whose readings we try to read. At a certain point (his double dream) the trauma of the Heights seems to burst into his sleeping mind. But only 'seems to': naturalistic explanation in terms of tapping of fir on pane denies us full access into the status of what has happened. Traumatized, his dreaming self enacts an atrocity, in a novel full of brutal reactions:

> Terror made me cruel; and, finding it useless to attempt shaking the creature off, I pulled its wrist on to the broken pane, and rubbed it to and fro till the blood ran down and soaked the bed-clothes: still it wailed, 'Let me in!' and maintained its tenacious gripe, almost maddening me with fear. (WH 23)

A sentence which begins with the word 'Terror' concludes in the word 'fear': a closed circle. The experience of visitation which Heathcliff would die for, Lockwood would kill to be rid of. Desire and terror are twin poles of human experience, forces generated by the identical object. Lockwood's dream causes Heathcliff to lose his guard. The vigil observed over half a lifetime by this apparently masterful man is broken, to reveal – a child. Bursting 'into an uncontrollable passion of tears':

'Come in! come in!' he sobbed. 'Cathy, do come. Oh do – *once* more! Oh! my heart's darling, hear me *this* time – Catherine, at last!' (*WH* 27)

For the first time we view the spasming, defenceless grief that underlies Heathcliff's defensive tension. The text has until this moment preserved a rigid detachment, through mockery, irony, Lockwood's veneer of *politesse*: now emotional lava briefly wells through a rift in the guarded world, giving poetic intensity to pure 'anguish', 'a gush of grief'.

Wuthering Heights is commonly read as a Romantic or romantic love story. But if the novel activates our hearts' desires, it also brings to life the 'terror that made me cruel'. The binary imagination of Emily Brontë rooted terror and desire in a single source: the inhuman face of the girl at the window; the longing for our dead to come home, which also terrifies us.

Amy Tan's *The Hundred Secret Senses* is a book of ghosts which, to the Chinese–American sister, are fearful and repellent, but, to the American–Chinese sister, cordial and benign. It records the binary, two-way ambiguity of the Chinese language:

> *Yi-ha-liu-si*: Miss Banner said it was like saying: Lose hope, slide into death. And I said, No, it means: Take hope, the dead remain. Chinese words are good and bad this way, so many meanings, depending on what you hold in your heart.[1]

Chinese is not unique in its ability to beckon and repel ghosts in one and the same sentence, double-bound in two-faced meaning which depends on the creative reader to construe. In the face of ambivalence, we often take sanctuary in casting out the undesired meaning, only to have it return by the other window. A key to understanding *Wuthering Heights* is precisely this: *Yi-ha-liu-si*. The crosswinds of its language create a force field of meaning, like that which double-binds Lockwood's mind upon entering the house, in his double dream of a chapel of mayhem, from which he wanted out, and a dead waif at the window, wanting in.

The novel has enduringly offered twin and opposite implications: *Lose hope, slide into death/Take hope, the dead remain.* But which do you choose? Once you have heard both, however, there is no final choice. Opt for one, and the rejected meaning haunts the word, mercilessly called up each time it is heard, like a *revenant*. Mutually exclusive meanings therefore defy a unilateral logic by implying one another. In turn, each alternative is itself dualistic: *lose hope, slide into death* seems negative but also suggests a yielding resolution of conflict in which the 'loss' of hope slips a tether binding one to life; *take hope, the dead remain* seems comforting, but is also disturbing, for if the dead cannot be safely buried, what hope is there for quiet nights?

Emily Brontë's mental world, its bias and compass defined by the Schlegelian 'ABER', 'yes but', is uniquely dialectical. The configuration 'both/and' rather than 'either/or' predominated. But, to push the dualist conundrum further, 'either/or' cannot be banished without bouncing back. Her natural mode is dialogue. In her novel of two narrators, in two volumes, there are two generations, two opposing houses, doubles, doubles of doubles, split personality, and a final tableau which, rather than solving all the problems, simply suspends them in eternal uncertainty. Is the eyewitnessing local lad right to see the *two* ghosts of 'Heathcliff and a woman, yonder, under t'Nab'; or is Lockwood right to see the *three* quarrellers – Catherine, Edgar, Heathcliff – at rest in 'this quiet earth'?

Amy Tan says that the interpretation you favour always depends on you; not reality. Reality is forever unknowable. 'So many meanings depend on what you hold in your heart'; 'You'll judge as well as I will, Mr Lockwood,' says Nelly, narrating to Lockwood, 'or you'll think you will, and that's as good.' A caustic reminder to the reader that you are on your own, make of it what you will. Emily Brontë slants her work askew by resting it on the destabilizing frame of irony – saying one thing, meaning (for all we know) the opposite, bringing all into a highly charged theatre of doubt. If each person's viewpoint is a cone of vision unique to himself, the reader is in a Berkeleyan dilemma of contending relativities.

Yet the novel is matter of fact, blunt, and down to earth. It detests cliché though it honours proverb. Nelly has charge of much of the tale. She does all possible to sabotage its Romanticism with, for instance, a no-nonsense Benthamite theory of human motivation and behaviour. Nelly's reiterated contention that individual action is based on self-interest and self-interest alone tends to be validated by the outcome of her predictions. Of the happiness in the Linton marriage, she observes: 'It ended. Well, we *must* be for ourselves in the long run; the mild and gentle are only more justly selfish than the domineering...' (*WH* 92); and again, she warns Catherine that Linton will only indulge her up to the point where 'something of equal consequence on both sides' splits their interests: 'and then those you term weak are very capable of being as obstinate as you' (*WH* 98). Nelly's brusquely rational calculation of the economy of interest has the force of a psychological law. Debit and credit must even up. Utilitarianism braces the novel against the extravagances of its characters' immortal but terminal loves and hates. But if matter of factness cold-shoulders these sublimities, it covertly permits us to indulge them. The repressed returns. Common sense objections are pre-empted, by being already omnipresent. The ironic mode of the novel arouses us to criticism of such emotional paucity.

The dialogue of prosaic narrative and poetic speech resembles a perpetual oscillation between conscious and unconscious minds; rational censorship against dream illumination. Nelly fusses round her charges and their aberrations, setting them to rights, as, for instance, Catherine shreds a pillow in her delirium, uttering one of the mightiest poetic speeches in our literature. Delivering the feathers of the dead birds whose lives have been sacrificed to make the pillow, she sorts them like Psyche and her seeds in the Greek myth:

> and this, I should know it among a thousand – it's a lapwing's. Bonny bird; wheeling over our heads in the middle of the moor. It wanted to get to its nest, for the clouds touched the swells, and it felt rain coming. This feather was picked up from the heath, the bird was not shot – we saw its nest in the winter full of little skeletons. Heathcliff set a trap over it, and the old ones dare not come....Did he shoot my lapwings, Nelly? Are they red, any of them? Let me look. (*WH* 122–3)

According to Nelly, Catherine is just making a mess. 'Give over with that baby-work', she nags, and, dragging the pillow away, turns '*the holes toward the mattress*, for she was removing the contents by handfuls' (*WH* 123, emphasis added). If, to Nelly, her wayward charge is making a mess, to us, she is declaring a revelatory truth. Cathy makes the pillow divulge and publicize its innards – shed lives of bird species, the cost of 'civilized' ease.

She also turns her mind inside out, to show us the depth of Heathcliff's damage and her affinity with the creatures of the heath. As she speaks, we imagine ourselves there, 'in the middle of the moors', and share a close-up view of the remains of the chicks and the parent birds' helpless aerial view. Our minds sadden for the creatures of earth, human and animal, young and old, and make the connection between the sentient nature with which Heathcliff has tampered, and the exposed children of the novel in their violated nest. Our minds extend and soar on the poetry of this vision, but are dumped back to earth by Nelly's colloquial intervention. What Nelly now enacts is a *cover-up*. She turns the pillow over, to bar Catherine from access to the holes, through which she has delivered her and our revelation. Thrift and sense impel the reinstatement of the comfortable as if it were the real. That way sanity lies.

But Nelly herself is double, duplicitous: her housekeeping can also involve mischief-making; her pietism leans to the platitudinous, but is shot through with the superstitious primitivism of country lore; her sympathies and antipathies are unstable. *Wuthering Heights* is composed of mutually challenging perspectives. If a book may be likened to a mind, *Wuthering Heights* is a mind radically at odds with itself.

It is full of secrets. Where did Heathcliff come from? Colourful suggestions abound: Linton thinks him 'a little Lascar, or an American or Spanish castaway', others label him 'gipsy'. How did he acquire his wealth and gentlemanly status: 'Did he finish his education on the Continent...? or did he get a sizar's place at College? or escape to America' and fight in the War of Independence? Or was he a highwayman? To Lockwood's fertile questions, Nelly answers that she hasn't a clue. A few pages later we learn that Hindley might know (*WH* 98), but, if so, we are kept in the dark. What was Cathy feeling during the period of her supposed 'happiness' with Edgar Linton? The novel, expressive as it is, is also repressive and tantalizing. It raises curiosity, to which it rations satisfaction. The inner narrator, Nelly, buries disagreeable truths and seeks to avoid hearing, for instance, Cathy's dream, which she heads off three times:

'I'm going to tell it....'
'Oh! don't, Miss Catherine' I cried. 'We're dismal enough without

conjuring up ghosts and visions to perplex us....'
'...I shall oblige you to listen...'
'I won't hear it! I won't hear it!'
'I tell you, I won't hearken to your dreams...'.   (WH 79–80)

Cathy tells her anyway. Or does she? Reading carefully, we discover that Cathy has selected *another* dream than the one she first had in mind, leaving the original untold. It remains in the realm of the unsaid.

What was the original dream? Who knows?

In this novel of many secrets, what is being repressed? Some taboo? Some unthinkable trespass which corresponds with the 'unforgivable sin' of Lockwood's first dream? Readers suspicious of an aura of unstated trespass, ascribe it to a buried incest at the novel's core.[2] It has been argued that Heathcliff is Mr Earnshaw's illegitimate offspring and hence Cathy's half-brother. Others have responded by emphasizing the curious sexlessness of the bond between Catherine and Heathcliff. The novel is treated as a code, which may one day be cracked, to reveal a meaning 'within' or 'beyond' itself. It is perceived as a communication with holes in which its secrets inhere. They are treated like pockets we can pick. But the truth is that the treasures we fetch out of them – such as Terry Eagleton's insistence that Heathcliff is an Irish immigrant[3] – were introduced in the first place by the triumphant discoverer.

For the holes in the telling *are* the meaning. They represent not just the costiveness of the author; nor an artistic device for keeping us guessing; they put us in touch at every point with the unaccountable, the not-told, the not-shown. On the one hand, they stand for pure loss. On the other, they imply the 'other world', the unknown from whose reaches we come and into whose uncanny silence the dead vanish. These two are linked. Deep and early loss is often uncommunicated because it is unspeakable. In the house of trauma, the 'wuthering' inhabitants are survivors of primary pain and rejection, and remain subject to a chronic panic of fear. If Heathcliff exhibits a manic power-lust, devouring Hindley's and Linton's heirs and estates, that is a sign of his weakness and insecurity. The little boy who promised to devote his whole life to 'paying him back' demanded 'Let me alone, and I'll plan it out; while I'm thinking of that, I don't feel pain' (WH 60). The more the adult Heathcliff masters and consumes his enemies, the emptier he grows, and the vaster swells the mnemonic of his loss mirrored across the whole face of the visible.

In Brussels, Emily Brontë had analysed the universe as 'a vast machine, constructed solely to produce destruction' ('The Butterfly', *BE* 178–9). In *Wuthering Heights* she analyses the mechanics and dynamics of a *system* (not merely an instance) of human damage. The family, unbalanced by the intrusion of the 'cuckoo in the nest', is anatomized as a microcosmic machine, fashioned in such a way that damage in one generation reproduces damage in the next. *Wuthering Heights* is a two-generational saga of child abuse, analysed as a process, in which the three 'H' characters are involved in cycles of retributive violence, so that each appears as substitute for the other. This dynamic displays a sardonic irony in Chapter XI, where Nelly's vivid recall of the innocent child Hindley, her early playmate, sends her haring to the Heights: and there she finds a real child, the duplicate of the phantom. 'The apparition had outstripped me'; but, no, she recognizes her mistake. This is 'Hareton, *my* Hareton'. Hareton greets his one-time nurse with a volley of curses and hurls a flint. The image of his father. Heathcliff has been wreaking revenge on Hindley through visiting on Hareton what Hindley had done to himself. Nelly sends him in to fetch his father, 'but, instead of Hindley, Heathcliff appeared...'. While writing this summary, my mind has been conscious of reeling with these systematic substitutions and reproductions. The three become indistinguishable, like a sequence of automata fated to circle on a clock, identical and programmed.

All these duplications seem to gesture back to an original and violated human condition, summed up in the image of the sleeping motherless baby, Hareton, above whose rest Nelly sings the grimmest of lullabies:

> It was far in the night, and the bairnies grat,
> The mither beneath the mools heard that.

> (WH 76)

The song of the awakened dead mother in the earth is a primitive Danish ballad, 'The Ghaists Warning', which Emily Brontë had found in the Appendix to Scott's *The Lady of the Lake* (1810). A stepmother withdraws light, food, heat from a family of seven motherless children:

> The bairns they stood wi' dule and doubt, –
> She up wi' her foot, and she kicked them out.

> Nor ale nor mead to the bairnies she gave.
> 'But hunger and hate frae me ye's have.'

> . . . . . .
> 'Twas lang i' the night, and the bairnies grat:
> Their mither she under the mools heard that.

The mother, dragged from her grave by her children's weeping, returns as a corpse, to comb, dress and dandle them, suckling the baby from her decayed breast. Terror and desire cohere in this eruptive image: the world beyond makes terrifying but benign assault on an earth crueller than anything underground. The stepmother is terrified into doing her duty to her unwanted charges, especially when the dog is heard howling in the night, a sign of the approach of the dead:

> Aye when they heard the dog nirr and bell,
> Sae ga'e they the bairnies bread and ale.

> Aye when the dog did wow, in haste
> They cross'd and sain'd themselves fraw the ghaist.

> Aye when the little dog yowl'd, with fear
> They shook at the thought that the dead was near.

This macabre ballad draws together the instinctual life of household beasts and the demonic world brooding beneath the mools ('the mould'). Animal instinct sniffs and heralds the proximity of nemesis, as the dog is heard to 'nirr', 'bell', 'wow', and 'yowl'. The dog–demon, subhuman–superhuman interface of ballad is the juncture on which *Wuthering Heights* calls up its ghosts. Nelly's macabre quotation over the sleeping Hareton speaks into a world whose children are rejects or orphans and get, at best, makeshift foster care.

Thus hair-raisingly blessed, Hareton smiles in his secure sleep: 'Look at little Hareton – *he's* dreaming nothing dreary. How sweetly he smiles in his sleep.'

'Yes; and how sweetly his father curses him in his solitude,' Catherine retorts. 'You remember him, I dare say, when he was just such another as that chubby thing – nearly as young and innocent' (*WH* 79). We grow to see the children of the novel as duplications, mirrorings of a universal condition, their cradle-quiet giving way to violent abuse. In this sense, Heathcliff is Hindley is Hareton.

For the mothers die. *Wuthering Heights* is a landscape of childhood grief and loss; an orphaned earth where mother-love is nowhere to be found. In a novel of rhythmic echoes of valediction, Frances dies after giving birth to Hareton: 'she put her two hands about his [Hindley's] neck, her face changed, and she was dead', leaving to Nelly her 'first bonny nursling' (*WH* 65). At the centre of the novel Catherine dies, giving birth to Nelly's second nursling: 'About twelve o'clock, that night, was born the Catherine you saw at Wuthering Heights, a puny, seven months' child; and two hours after the mother died, having never recovered sufficient consciousness to miss Heathcliff, or know Edgar' (*WH* 164). Common in eighteenth and nineteenth century England, motherlessness in Emily Brontë's world is comprehensive. Her own experience of mother-loss is projected out upon the planet as universal catastrophe. Constantly, the novel reaches back to origins – and finds them in loss. Romantic love is an attempt to breach the fatal flaw in the creation; and that flaw is not simply a marginal theme but a primary subject of *Wuthering Heights*. The author views creaturely life as a continuum, from humans to dogs, birds, and past these to grass, trees, stones, wind. The life-spirit flows through all and is to be respected in all; but the same mortal flaw is imprinted everywhere. The novel is a requiem for humanity and nature.

When Heathcliff hears of Cathy's death, he has been outside in the park all night:

> leant against an old ash tree, his hat off, and his hair soaked with the dew that had gathered on the budded branches, and fell pattering round him. He had been standing a long time in that position, for I saw a pair of ousels passing and repassing scarcely three feet from him, busy in building their nest, and regarding his proximity no more than that of a piece of timber. (*WH* 165–6)

The piercing beauty of this tableau (with its pair-bonded alliterations, 'budded branches', 'busy in building') is in direct measure to its pain. Thrushes, building for the new season's young, mistake the stockstill Heathcliff for a rooted part of the sylvan scene: like the old ash that pours onto his barrenness the irony of purifying dewfall. Nelly's description of Catherine's passing ('She drew a sigh, and stretched herself, like a child reviving...' (*WH* 166)) recalls Frances's death.

Heathcliff's savage requiem, 'May she wake in torment...', has an operatic magnitude of emotion:

> Be with me always – take any form – drive me mad! only *do* not leave me in this abyss, where I cannot find you! Oh, God! it is unutterable! I *cannot* live without my life! I *cannot* live without my soul!   (*WH* 167)

It is the child's original rage of loss of the being on whom existence depends: and the child's refusal of assent to finality. Neither Heathcliff nor Catherine has ever recovered from mother-loss enough to create an independent identity. Being one another's 'all-in-all', all is lost with the other's removal. These are weaklings, with mighty cravings and the voices and imaginations of poets. Edgar Linton is more himself than they are themselves. The ousels and lapwings are not simply metaphor, decoration, setting, for these human events. They, and their habitat, with its fertility and blight, are part of the subject matter of the novel, 'background' pulled to 'foreground', margin to centre.

Heathcliff demands 'Where is she?' He has no conception of 'nowhere'. Catherine must be elsewhere, in 'another world', the possibility of which the novel constantly raises, spectrally locating it fugitively somewhere in the earth, beyond it, on the earth, within the heart of the invisible. But the Christian heaven, that 'other world' in which Nelly trusts, has neither meaning nor reality to the antinomian lovers. God and Satan are equally their enemies. Yet death is also a dash for home; a refuge and escape. 'He's safe,' (*WH* 294) is how the second Catherine describes Linton Heathcliff's death, and the doctor speaks of Hindley's death as 'giv[ing] us the slip'. Catherine looks forward to dwelling in a 'glorious world' beyond this earth; yet her earlier dream refuses a transcendent world in favour of the heathlands below. 'None would ask a Heaven | More like this Earth than thine,' wrote Emily Brontë in a poem of 1841, 'Shall Earth no more inspire thee'. If the stress of inner conflict in 'this shattered prison' makes death a longed-for retreat, 'How beautiful the earth is still', as another poem affirms, and the energy of the writing in *Wuthering Heights* attests. Besides, in

Emily Brontë's dualistic universe, abdication might be into an arena just as restless and unsatisfied as this one. Who knows?

Yi-ha-liu-si: Lose hope, slide into death.
Yi-ha-liu-si: Take hope, the dead remain.

Both interpretations are betrayed by inner ambivalences. The structure of *Wuthering Heights* has been compared with a nest of Chinese boxes, which forbid certain distinction between outside and inside[4] and admit you to a centre of emptiness. In this tissue of hidden meanings, even the title is a conundrum.

Nobody in England knew much about the meteorology of 'wuthering' until 1847. Emily Brontë introduced the word into our culture, and felt bound to explain its dialect meaning, in guide book fashion, on the second page: 'Wuthering Heights is the name of Mr Heathcliff's dwelling, "Wuthering" being a significant provincial adjective, descriptive of the atmospheric tumult to which its station is exposed in stormy weather.' Emily plucked the word from Yorkshire dialect, the same rich word-hoard as Joseph's dialect, requiring translation into standard English, transcribed phonetically. Joseph's language is in vociferous dispute with the southern-gentry dialect of the text and major characters. The author teases the reader to crack his code, and relish his words' flinty rasp on our tongues as we 'translate':

> 'Wah!' answered Joseph, 'yon dainty chap says he cannut ate 'em [porridge]. Bud Aw guess it's raight! His mother were just soa – we were a'most too mucky tuh sow t'corn fur makking her breead.' (*WH* 209)

Rude sounds (*Wah!*) mock the affectations of effete Lintonism; vowels stretch to blasting diphthongs (*soa, breead*); standard English contracts (*'em, a'most, t'corn*); a breed and class of men makes its stand against the polite discourse of the narrative voices. An indispensable class, without which the gentry cannot eat. Joseph evokes and directs our laughter: his language is canny. He talks back against the mealy-mouthed, Frenchified lispings of the speakers of polite English, complaining with screwed-up nose in disgusted parody, that he can't follow Isabella's mouthings:

> Mim! Mim! Mim! Did iver Christian body hear owt like it? Minching

un' munching! Hah can Aw tell whet ye say? (*WH* 138)

Hah indeed? Once we have worked out Joseph's meaning, we find he is protesting that he cannot work out what *we* are saying. For most middle-class readers speak the same standard English as Isabella, and, according to Joseph's norms, all such speakers are outlandish. They talk a foreign language. When Isabella wants to know where the 'parlour' is, Joseph mimics again: '*Parlour!... parlour!* Nay, we've no *parlours.*' She can have a sarcastic conducted tour of t'rahms but will not find a *parlour.* And at '*Bed-rumes!*' he is off again. The word 'Wuthering', then, does not originate in couth, literary English, but in a language *within* spoken English, which thrives aggressively on the uplands where the heather does. 'Wuthering' is not originally a sublime word. Emily Brontë invokes it to create atmospherics – both vernacular and foreign, uncouth and impressive – modifying the Romantic preoccupation with solitude at altitude, wild vistas, and 'atmospheric tumult'.

How translatable is *Wuthering Heights*? Translation into foreign languages places problems of interpretation under high magnification and focuses attention on the fine detail. For all reading (even within our own language) is a form of translation, in which, to explain a meaning, we substitute an alternative set of words. That conversion leads inexorably away from the original words toward deviant meanings. The first translation of *Wuthering Heights* into a foreign language was (aptly) the German translation of 1851, entitled *Wutheringshöhe, 'Ein Roman von Ellis Currer Bell'*, in three volumes. The anonymous translator made no effort to translate 'wuthering' into a German equivalent, allowing Lockwood's explanation to gloss the word. In 1938 Ingrid Rambach, attempting to root the word more firmly in the soil of German language, called it *Die Sturmhöhe* ('Storm-heights'), which Ingrid Rein followed in her 1986 *Sturmhöhe.* French translations came later, with Frederic Delebecque's *Les Hautes de Hurle-Vent* ('The Heights of Roaring Wind') of 1925; Jacques and Yolande de Lacretelle's *Haute-Plainte* ('High-Lament') of 1927; Sylvère Monod's *Hurlement* ('Roaring') of 1963. A modern Italian translation called the novel *Cime tempestose.* 'Storm', 'tempest', 'lament', 'high wind': nothing quite as wuthering as 'Wuthering', with its present participle enacting a continuous turbulence, its closeness to 'weathering'.

The German *Sturmhöhe* comes close to the compression of the title: German's facility in the generation of compound nouns realizes the compact and abrupt strength of Emily Brontë's title – but without dialectal flavour. *Sturm* is as common and obvious a word as 'Wuthering' is unexpected and localized. 'The Heights of Roaring Wind' loosens the taut title, but incorporates both the sense of height and gale; 'Roaring' has abrupt power but we lose the sense of height. Reading Emily Brontë's novel in translation yields a strange impression of wandering *near* a familiar path, which one is destined never to tread – yet of gaining from this adjacent track advantage, if not of access, then of viewpoint.

In *Wuthering Heights*, as in the finest poetry, every word tells, together with word order, paragraphing, and punctuation. Consider, for instance, the famous ending, in which Lockwood contemplates the graves of Catherine, Edgar Linton, and Heathcliff:

> I lingered round them, under that benign sky; watched the moths fluttering among the heath, and hare-bells; listened to the soft wind breathing through the grass; and wondered how any one could ever imagine unquiet slumbers for the sleepers in that quiet earth.   (WH 338)

Here is the conclusion of the 1851 German translation, *Wutheringshöhe*. Lockwood wonders:

> *wie irgend Jemand denken konnte, dass der Schlummer der Schläfer in jener stillen Erde unruhig sein könne.*[5]

Serviceable enough, but, though it preserves a wraith of the original music in the alliteration of *Schlummer* and *Schläfer*, the sentence has no choice but to decline in a conditional auxiliary verb, 'could', rather than repose in 'that quiet earth'.

The 1986 *Sturmhöhe* tackles problems of meaning, word order, and cadencing thus:

> *wie jemand auf den Gedanken kommen könnte, die Schläfer in diesem stillen Fleckchen Erde ruhten nicht in Frieden.*[6]

The modern translator (with the twentieth-century loosening of word-order constraints) transacts the weakening tangle of verbs earlier, in order to move towards an equivalent 'quiet ending', achieving this not in the original word 'earth', the destination of the whole of *Wuthering Heights*, but in 'peace'. The ambivalence of the construction of the final clauses, which, by wondering how anyone could imagine unquiet slumbers, raises the ghost of a possibility that someone very well might, is over-emphasized in 'ruhten nicht in Frieden'. The negative article does not appear in the original, which balances *unquiet* against *quiet*. Finally, 'ein Fleckchen Erde', 'a spot of earth' fails to reproduce the English 'earth', for it dissects a portion of the planet rather than returning the three mortals to original totality.

Finally, here is Ingrid Rambach's 1938 German translation, which wonders:

> *was den letzten Schlummer der Schläfer in diesem stillen Stückchen Erde stören konnte.*[7]

Schlummer and *Schläfer* are balanced against alliterations of *stillen*, *Stückchen* and *stören*, with the effect of a tongue-twister. Here, the translator's excess reminds us of Emily's essentially light poetic touch.

Sylvère Monod's *Hurlement* concludes with 'dormeurs qui reposent en cette terre tranquille' and Anna Zazo's Italian *Cime tempestuose* determines 'in quella terra serena'.[8] Vernacular word order has allowed both to resolve in the 'quiet earth' of the original, but at the cost of placing the adjective 'quiet' as the conclusive emphasis.

I felt in reading over these translations the genuine exertion of each translator to reproduce the poetry of Emily Brontë's classic ending, its carefully modulated cadencing as it comes to rest in – not a dying fall – but a reposeful balance of eternally suspended contradictions. I was drawn back to the precise composition of the final sentence (which is also one whole paragraph). 'I lingered...watched...listened...wondered': the fourfold music of these verbs struck my inner ear, the alternating 'l' and 'w' alliterations, the assonantal and rhythmic echo of 'lingered' in 'wondered'. The last paragraph is a lyrical meditation which formally lays to rest the discordant actions in the reader's mind. We too linger and wonder over its mysteriously beautiful unfolding. I noticed the near-chiasmus in the close: 'unquiet : slumbers : : sleepers : quiet', the form reversing itself in a final arabesque. I 'watched' the mental images that arose, and 'listened' to their gentle echoes: 'heath' evokes Heathcliff; in 'hare-bells' murmur the names of Hareton, Ellen, and Isabella. The wind does not blow but is heard 'breathing', like a living spirit. Finally: 'this quiet earth'. Wherever one intuits the characters have gone, these words bring the story to an andante, pianissimo conclusion, homing to the place of origins.

But the translations I have read terminate in anything but 'earth'. Word order and usage in other languages impose constraints translation cannot break without absurdity. Yet each translator honourably labours for equivalents to the poetry of the original. At best, they produce a memorial, each substituted word having its fingers at its lips, bidding adieu.

And perhaps this is all anyone can do for this text of homesickness, of reluctant valediction; a text which turns from its reader, fugitive or cold-shouldering. Criticism memorializes a bygone adventure as the eye traverses the text in its rhythmic roving from line to line. But the story carries its own imperatives, teaching us how to read, just before it is too late: 'linger ...watch...listen...wonder...'. Receptive surrender, allowing the words to go 'through and through' us, altering 'the colour of our minds', is the route to understanding. Cathy's proviso: 'I cannot express it but...' is also a guide. *Wuthering Heights* requires two readers: the receptive one who listens, as we do to music, allowing the poetry to wash through and through her, and the dynamic reader who wonders, queries, argues, pits her wits against the novel's abstruseness.

Wuthering Heights spoke first to a German readership: Germany was quick to grasp the secret that Emily had been quick to grasp in German literature. What in English fiction was new and astonishing had, in Germany, been recognized for fifty years: *Sturm und Drang*, the demonic *Doppelgänger*, dualism, the primacy of the inner mind, the brother–sister bond, and perhaps especially the *Liebestod* or the *Todeserotik* in which the dead beloved becomes the unconscious self of the lover, had been current for decades. Novalis at the grave of Sophie von Kühn, notoriously proclaimed: 'with her the whole world has died for me. Since then I have not belonged to the world.' Romantic morbidity, equating mound with marriage-bed, in that equivocal 'other world' which lies beyond the visible and within the imagining mind, was dramatized by Novalis's consummations at young Sophie's graveside: 'In the evenings I went to Sophie. I was indescribably joyful there – flashing moments of enthusiasm – I blew the grave away in front of me like dust – centuries were like moments – I could feel her nearness – I believed she would appear at any moment.'[9] From Novalis to Heathcliff at the grave of Catherine 'I felt her by me – I could *almost* see her and yet I *could not!' (WH* 290)) is no great journey for the German Romantic sensibility. Yet Novalis (who was a real person) in his unequivocal ecstasy seems less real, more facile, than Heathcliff (mere fiction) in the naked authenticity of grief, with its anguish of loss denial. The German theme of homesickness (*Sehnsucht, Heimweh,* gracefully articulated in Goethe's song, 'Mignon', familiar to Emily in several sources) is also a key theme of *Wuthering Heights,* and merges with the *Liebestod* theme. Goethe's land where the golden oranges glow in the dark foliage like lamps of memory represents a world beyond, elsewhere – an eternal Italy of the imagination:

> *Kennst du das Land, wo die Zitronen blühn?*
> *Im dunkeln Laub die Gold-Orangen glühn,*
> *Ein sanfter Wind vom blauen Himmel weht,*
> *Die Myrte still und hoch der Lorbeer steht,*
> *Kennst du es wohl?*
> > *Dahin! dahin!*
> *Möcht ich mit dir, o mein Geliebter, ziehn.*

'Dahin' – 'there, over there' – is almost as important to *Wuthering Heights* as Schlegel's 'ABER' – 'yes but'. The homesick longing for exclusive reunion with the lost in a world somewhere just beyond where we are standing is a craving of the whole novel. Edgar Linton, the least 'mystical' of the characters, 'lying, through long June evenings, on the green mound of [Cathy's] mother's grave, and wishing, yearning for the time when I might lie beneath it' (*WH* 257), continues his marriage after his wife's death by literally lying on top of her, his body as near to hers as earth can suffer it to come. The verbs 'wishing, yearning' denote a chord to which the novel endlessly recurs. And as it expresses abandonment to longing, so it arouses vestiges of such longing in its readers.

If *Wutheringshöhe* in 1851, four years after *Wuthering Heights* had been published, could only partially realize the voice of its original, it was still, in a genuine way, taking the novel home. German Protestant tradition was peculiarly well placed to translate, if not the regional dialect, the religiosity of Joseph, since the Lutheran and Calvinist inheritance of the German-speaking countries found the figure instantly recognizable. '"Gott stehe uns bei!" murmelte er' – '"The Lord help us!" he soliloquized, in a tone of peevish displeasure' (*WH* 2). In German-speaking Europe, the anabaptists and antinomians who were Joseph's spiritual ancestors were native-bred. He stands in violent dispute but covert analogy with Catherine and Heathcliff, in 'piking out' the 'chozzen' from 'th'rubbidge'. His manic misogyny and punitive agenda sound out a tremendous comic bass – a sublime oompah – to the storm at the Heights, in a novel by a woman, antagonistic to the patriarchal Almighty. Jehovah is represented solely by a vanishing curate, a decaying church, the 491-part sermon of the Reverend Jabes Branderham in Lockwood's dream – and Joseph. Excise Joseph and one of the novel's cornerstones keels down. He appears or is mentioned or quoted in nearly every chapter: the 'old ruffian', the 'old sinner', grumbles his way through both generations, and, as he was there from the first, so he will be there at the last, when all other characters have fled, into marriage, civilization, or the earth.

'I *cannot* live without my life! I *cannot* live without my soul!' keens Heathcliff at Catherine's death. It should be simple enough to translate:

> *Wutheringshöhe*: 'Ich kann nich leben, ohne meinem Leben! Ich kann nicht leben, ohne meiner Seele!'

> *Sturmhöhe*: 'Ich *kann* nicht leben ohne meinem Leben! Ich *kann* nicht leben ohne meiner Seele!'

How weak the first appears beside the second, which follows the original notation. In failing to observe Emily Brontë's italicization, it resembles the mistranscription of a musical score from the composer's original, omitting *forte* or *molto appassionata*, and hence failing to deliver to the reader's mind emphasis and mood. *Wuthering Heights* is rich in italicizations, occurring in speeches of maximum intensity. We might wonder why the author chose to make these explicit, since the speeches' highly wrought emotion, amounting to frenzy, makes tone obvious. Take them out and one sees why. In poetry, she would trust (though she did not always do so) that metre, rhyme, line position, would convey emphases. She could not trust prose that far:

> Cóme ín! cóme ín!... Cáthy, do cóme. Oh do – *once* more! Óh! my heárt's darling, heár me *this* time – Cátherine, át lást!' (WH 27).

Short, spasmodic phrasing; repetition (*come* three times, *Cathy/ Catherine, do...Oh do...Oh*); assonance (*heart's darling/last*); alliteration (Cathy/come, heart/hear) are not considered sufficient to create the desired effect of bursting passion. By emphasizing *once* and *this*, the author ensures that virtually the whole invocation is composed of stressed monosyllables. In normal English, you can't and don't stress everything. Only a baby's cry stresses every syllable. This is the total cry of an infant. *Once* begs a single advent as a bargain for a lifetime vigil; *this* recalls a lifetime of calling 'do come'. And the cry apportioned between the imperative and plea of 'do' and 'come' (with their terrible shadows, 'don't' and 'go') echoes across the whole novel: 'Oh, don't, don't go. It is the last time! Edgar will not hurt us. Heathcliff, I shall die! I shall die!' (*WH* 162) are Cathy's last words on earth.

Heathcliff's savage invocation after her death also stresses 'do': 'Be with me always... only *do* not leave me in this abyss, where I cannot find you!' Emily Brontë's italicization of his 'I *cannot...cannot...*' hence expresses not only an ecstasy of pain, in crescendo of protest, but what Catherine had expressed as the 'impracticability' of separating the two of them. The emphases imprint upon the reader's mind patterns of extreme need, unmediated and primal. Sentences in these breathless speeches are linked on dashes, abdicating the nuanced grammar of comma, colon, semi-colon, full stop, in which literary language gravely measures the length and status of its pauses. In this stampeding world of emotion, there is no time for such notation. The breathings of the voice under stress are explicitly pitted *against* the passage of time. Time bereaves. To consent to move on with time, to heal and mature, would be to admit the irrevocable passing of the loved person. Cathy has already conceived the possibility of Heathcliff's recovery:

> Will you forget me – will you be happy when I am in the earth? Will you say twenty years hence [i.e. the 'now' of the narrative] 'That's the grave of Catherine Earnshaw. I loved her long ago and was

wretched to lose her; but it is past. I've loved others since – my children are dearer to me than she was, and, at death, I shall not rejoice that I am going to her, I shall be sorry that I must leave them!' Will you say so, Heathcliff?   (*WH* 158–9)

Premonition of eternal solitude in the earth, with the fantasy of self-aware burial, launches this attack on Heathcliff's possible survival and maturation. The desire *never to be parted* impels a vindictive passion which refuses not only the wounds but also the blessings of time. 'Time stagnates here,' meditates Lockwood at the Heights. In the house of trauma, nobody ever grows up, passes through, or comes to terms with the travail of loss. We see in Heathcliff a grief that is eternal, and a man who is a rejected and bereaved child, immortally. The novel is scored for the voice, to help its readers to breathe its rhythms in the mind as they read and hence to put us in touch with the deepest areas of the unconscious.

> So runs my dream: but what am I?
> An infant crying in the night:
> An infant crying for the light:
> And with no language but a cry.[10]

Tennyson's mellifluous 'In Memoriam' captures and describes but belies the breakdown of utterance under the horror of grief. The word *infant* derives from the Latin word, *infans*, 'languageless'. Tennyson crafts and calms a passion in the cradle of rocking, measured rhythm. Emily Brontë creates a language capable of expressing the visceral. She lays bare the child in her people and in the reader: the spirit-girl at the window of our eyes, saying 'Let me in'.

Wuthering Heights is therefore minutely notated for inward performance within the reading mind. It insists on the scrupulous ordering of its incendiary materials. Examination of Emily Brontë's sheet music revealed concern for the minutiae of distinction of emphasis, time, mood, and technical precision. Just as finicking attention to detail produces a virtuoso pianist, so attention to rhythm, punctuation, stress, and word order produces a virtuoso text, however stormy – and a virtuoso reader, willing to co-create the novel in the mind. Romanticism had a concept of the 'active' and 'passive' reader, which predates the reader theory of the 1980s by nearly two centuries, Schlegel's 'synthetic writer' who 'constructs and creates his own reader...not...resting and dead, but lively and advancing towards him'. This dynamic (as opposed to mechanistic) writer solicits a dynamic reader, who he tempts 'to do the inventing for himself'.[11] The idea that books generate readers who complete the text through their cooperative creativity takes us aback by its modernity. *Wuthering Heights* uniquely arouses the 'creative reader' in us: not because it is a wild novel but because of its strenuous control, detachment, and obedience to self-evolved laws.

Passion alternates with prosaism; flights of melody with terse telling which gets a move on and does not suffer the flighty gladly. Like lightning earthed, Catherine's tempestuous poetry ('I am Heathcliff...') bundles its burning face into Nelly's apron, which, however, she jerks away, for 'I was out of patience with her folly!' (*WH* 82). The range of diction and register is remarkable, the extraordinary homing inexorably to the ordinary, abstract to solid. Unmediated storm and stress would soon pall. Antiphonal relationships prevail, like alternations of recitative and aria in opera. Scepticism bathes the whole narrative in irony. Heroics mirror themselves as maladaptive flouncings; grandeur as folly. Yet the ironies, in this canny novel, turn ironically upon themselves. In subverting, they certify.

So does the solidity of furniture and the reliability of daily life. The black press, the great dresser, green-painted chairs, the white floor, a maid at the hearth raking cinders, Zillah with a frying pan, named dogs licking up spilt porridge, Joseph spreading lime. Imaginative space is totally inhabited and known; and it gives on to real space. Charlotte Brontë noted with amusement that 'Parry's Palace' (Emily's residence in the Brontë children's play world) lacked a certain sumptuous *je ne sais quoi*. It seemed only half in the fantasy world, being fitted out with wash-house, 'back kitchin stable & coal house': otherwise how could Emily's imaginary people survive? Charlotte, accustomed to a glamorous imaginative norm, found the goings on madly banal. All they did at Parry's was eat mashed potato, Yorkshire pudding, apple pie, and cucumber, causing her guest, the explorer Ross (Anne), to throw up so violently as to require magical intervention.[12] When the children invented giants ten miles high, Emily stubbornly

limited hers to four miles.[13] Had shrewd Dr Johnson materi-
alized to object that anyone who could imagine a four-mile-
high man could manage six miles extra, Emily might have
mentioned propriety of limits. Her people in *Wuthering Heights*
are sky-aspirers – but their hands need washing, their porridge
cooking (with or without lumps), and a huge bellows must be
provided, as well as a box of matches, before the fire – however
symbolic – can be got going. When Heathcliff flings a tureen of
apple sauce at his rival, Edgar's face is scrubbed with 'a
dishcloth'; when Cathy strews feathers, they have to be cleared
up, to the tune of mithering: 'There's a mess! The down is flying
about like snow!'

Nelly chides, sets to rights, and scales down the measure of
the sky-aspirers: 'our fiery Catherine was no more than a wailing
child!' she gloats. Yet this scaling-down also sets off a contradictory tendency. When Nelly speaks of the down from the
pillow 'flying about like snow', she unconsciously implies
blizzard conditions within the warm room and her image
reverberates with Cathy's throwing-open of the casement:
'careless of the frosty air that cut about her shoulders keen as
a knife' (*WH* 126). Equally, Nelly's sneering reduction of
'ma'am' to 'a wailing child' calls up our memory of that icy-
handed girl-spirit, who called herself 'Catherine Linton' and
'sobbed', 'replied shiveringly', 'wailed', 'mourned' at the
window of Lockwood's sleep. Nelly's scaling-down often works
in this binary way: it reinforces what it denies. Artistically, the
technique is at once tactful and licentious. It allows the author to
indulge, without embarrassment, preposterous, hundred-mile-
high ascents of imagination. Inflation and deflation, by authorial
sleight, are hand in glove. Nelly's value judgements do not
dominate us but pre-empt our making the same negative,
common sense criticisms. She doesn't like Catherine, but then
we may not take to Nelly. Emily Brontë's craft beguiles her
reader into searching for meanings, constantly on the loose.

Because of its drive and conciseness, *Wuthering Heights* is
sometimes thought of as a novel founded in a pithy Anglo-
Saxon-derived lexis. In fact, its vocabulary is far more copious
and literary than we may be aware as we read, carried along by
the thrust of the telling. If I list some of the synonyms for the
functional 'said' in dialogue, this wide, bookish reach comes into

focus. Crisp and economical in the telling, *Wuthering Heights* is verb- and noun-founded, with sparing use of adjectives and adverbs; hence the compulsive volition of the action. But, while never ornate, vocabulary is often Latinate and polysyllabic. The author precipitates speech as action, so that words in dialogue (and dialogue in this novel is overwhelmingly quarrel) suggest *things* that are being *pitched* at the hearer. Verbs defining speech-acts have momentum and energy. They include:

asseverated (several instances)
answered/replied/retorted
vociferated
expostulated
affirmed (many instances)/*declared*
remarked
responded
whispered
sobbed/cried/broke out (common)
vow
commenced
shouted
exclaimed (very common)
grated out, gasped, muttered, croaked, snarled, screamed through
    his nose (Joseph)
observed
ejaculated
hallooed
continued/added/persevered/persisted
snapped
interrupted/interposed
inquired
returned (common, implying antagonism)
demanded (common)
soliloquised
begged
hold communion with (Heathcliff, Cathy I)
converse
ventured
abjured

Verbs notably absent in my scan were of the *suggested, implied* ilk. Characters in the novel are prone to insist on their feeling or point of view, affirming, ejaculating, exclaiming; they do not ask, they demand; they do not modify or subtilize their view, they repeat, continue, persevere in maintaining the view they always had. The tentative is eschewed in favour of all-out war. Compromise is unknown to most of the characters. Because they are eternally bickering, and one quarrel engenders another, their words retaliate on one another as do their deeds:

> 'For shame! for shame!' [Isabella] *repeated*, angrily. 'You are worse than twenty foes, you poisonous friend!'
> 'Ah! you won't believe me, then?' *said* Catherine. 'You think I speak from wicked selfishness?'
> 'I'm certain you do,' *retorted* Isabella; 'and I shudder at you!'
> 'Good!' *cried* the other...
> 'And I must suffer for her egotism!' she *sobbed* ... (WH 102–3)

Repeating, retorting, crying, sobbing, Emily Brontë's people carry the unmediated emotion of childhood into their adult lives, where it creates mayhem. Words wreak vocal violence, the equivalent of the 'shower of terrific slaps on both sides of the head' which are Heathcliff's mode of communication with the second Cathy (WH 271). For Joseph's dialect speeches, which typically take the form of cryptic tirade or caustic curse, Emily Brontë reserves a rich hoard of comic verbs expressive of his croaking, gasping, grating, screaming, and nasalizations. Nelly neutralizes the explosive utterances of the performers by her more common *said, observed, replied*.

The text's recurrent Latinity is a complex phenomenon. We register the irony latent in Lockwood's polite polysyllabics, as he demands to be let out of the Heights, uttering 'several incoherent threats of retaliation that, in their indefinite depth of virulency, smacked of King Lear' (WH 16). This pocket-sized Lear with his long words for little things is swept up in the palm of the author's hand and surveyed with amusement, as the 'vehemence of my agitation' erupts in a humiliating nosebleed. The suave assurance of her style is exemplified in deftness of phrasing: 'indefinite depth of virulency', implying ease within a large cultural background. But poor Lockwood's *retaliation* is soon dumped down by the comic genius of the author into the childish bathos of mere 'scolding'. It is embattled Zillah, the erstwhile saviour with the frying pan, whose exertions with that implement had quelled the 'storm' of dogs, leaving her stout bosom 'heav[ing] like a sea after a high wind' (*WH* 5), who again masters the uproar. She 'turns her vocal artillery' against Hareton. The mock-heroic art of the author sets highly literary style against plain speech, dialect vibrating against standard English. Dialect enters the lucubrations of the text like a door banged open by a gale: 'Wisht, wisht! you munn't go on so – come in, and I'll cure that. There now, hold ye still.'

Wuthering Heights is concerned with books and reading, to which it preserves a double attitude. Linton's library is his retreat from a world he cannot control. The second Cathy triumphs over Heathcliff by rendering Hareton literate. We know of Emily Brontë's omnivorous passion for reading. Heathcliff, denied books, is degraded, but books of edification are anathema: 'I took my dingy volume by the scroop,' records Cathy in her diary, 'and hurled it into the dog-kennel, vowing I hated a good book.' This is the sole recorded instance of the word *scroop* in English literature, but the *Oxford English Dictionary* may be wrong in suggesting that Emily Brontë used it by mistake for 'scruff'. Just as possibly, *scroop* may be an unrecorded dialect word, native to her home locality. The novel's vigour owes much to its ability to draw on the pith of oral, untranscribed speech. *Scroop* associates the spine of a book with the scruff of a dog's neck: Joseph's book is treated as a ruffian and *hurled* (not *thrown* or *deposited*) into the proper place for a beast, the dog kennel. Heathcliff, in a paragraph of seven well-aimed words, kicks his into the same goal. In the sabbath hell that reigns in Hindley's parlour (the newly-weds meanwhile basking in paradisal hearth warmth), Joseph's ministry to the good-for-nothings conceives in them a loathing of all things improving as a form of torture against which the self-respecting spirit rebels.

Cathy's diary, however, in which this incident is memoralized, includes another register of language:

> 'An awful Sunday!... I wish my father were back again. Hindley is a *detestable substitute* – his conduct to Heathcliff is *atrocious* – H. and I are going to rebel – we took our *initiatory* step this evening...
>
> My *companion* is impatient and proposes that we should *appropriate* the dairy woman's cloak, and have a scamper on the moors, under its shelter. A pleasant suggestion – and then, if the surly old man

come in, he may believe his *prophecy verified* – we cannot be damper, or colder, in the rain than we are here. (*WH* 18, 20; emphasis added).

The text of Cathy's diary oscillates between high-handed polysyllable and raw child-speech. Cathy's English is child-prodigy level when evaluating her brother as a *detestable substitute* for her father and recording an *initiatory step* rather than 'a first step'. The pair do not propose to 'take' or 'filch' the dairywoman's cloak, in that haunting image, but *appropriate* it, with a grand sense of taking command of the article. Neither is Heathcliff my 'friend' but *my companion*. Cathy has raided Joseph's Calvinist lexicon for the contempt and rancour with which she conceives Joseph imagining his *prophecy verified*. Joseph had *asseverated* (another prodigy-word) that ' "owd Nick" would fetch us as sure as we were living'. Such high-register words imbue Cathy's text with caustic irony. They frame a haughty manner which is apt to her character but questionable for her age-group. These ink-horn terms stand in contrast with the simple and vivid 'awful Sunday', the 'scamper' on the moors, the sense of cold, wet children that echoes forlornly (though the two are not sorry for themselves) in her final phrase. The author has allocated to her young character elevated diction from her own mental hoard, to suggest a tragi-comic campaign of rebellion on the part of ill-used children. Captive princes and princesses in Gondal had known one another as 'Companions', escaping from the palaces of Instruction as Cathy and Heathcliff escape the attic of theology. Perhaps a modicum of the vocabulary familiar to the Gondalian aristos spilled over into the Yorkshire of *Wuthering Heights*.

The boy Heathcliff's account of their peep into the Thrushcross window at the Linton children presents something of the same verbal contrariety. Having informed Nelly that she'll have to 'seek for [Cathy's] shoes in the bog to-morrow', he goes on to describe the 'splendid palace carpeted with crimson... and a pure white ceiling bordered by gold, a shower of glass-drops hanging in silver chains...'. His hushed, exclamatory 'ah! it was beautiful' exhales a child's awe at first sight of a sumptuous interior, and the rhythms and idioms are precisely heard. 'We laughed outright at the petted things, we did despise them!' with the disgust of the spartan for the petulance of the privileged, quarrelling over a dog, the solidarity of the double *we*, the emphatic auxiliary, '*did* despise'. He mimes Isabella's and Edgar's bleating for mama and papa, but when the bulldog is let loose and bites Cathy's leg, the register changes: 'The devil had seized her ankle, Nelly; I heard his *abominable* snorting.... I *vociferated* curses enough to *annihilate* any fiend in *Christendom*, and I got a stone and thrust it between his jaws, and tried with all my might to cram it down his throat' (*WH* 47). When Skulker is throttled off, Heathcliff follows them in 'grumbling *execrations*'. The reader may be forgiven for wondering what lad ever uttered *execrations* or *vociferated curses* in that studious way, rather than plain cursing and swearing? The passage (taken to task in an early review on account of its supposed 'vulgarity' and 'coarseness') occurs at a moment of maximum excitement, where the author again lends the resources of a sophisticated voice to the child-narrator. *Abominable* qualifies the dog's *snorting* as it hangs on to its human meat. *Vociferate* is a powerful Latinism, meaning to 'give voice to'. *Annihilate* tolls through the novel like a death knell. Meanwhile, the verbs *thrust* and *cram* carry the all-out, violent energy with which Catherine's companion seeks to choke off the creature. The description of its 'purple tongue hanging *half a foot* out of his mouth, and his pendant lips streaming with bloody slaver' measures and colours horror for the reader, with a kind of authorial relish. A final miniature, framed in the window, of Cathy pinching the nose of the dog as she eats up cakes at the fireside, with no hard feelings, is vividly seen and memorably simple in expression.

G. W. Peck in his review of 1848 was painfully exercised by the author's 'ill-mannered contempt for the decencies of language', advising that the author endeavour to 'eradicate his provincialism by taking lessons of a London footman'. Discussing the passages above, he maintains, in a self-confounding manner, that the occurrence of such 'examples of simple vulgarity, or want of a refined perception', in a work 'written with so much strength' are hardly noticed '(and thousands such) as blemishes' by the reader. But this, the purist maintains, 'does not redeem them'.[14]

Of course it does. If the narrative thrust established by the author's dynamic mode is so powerful that the reader's mind is unconscious of 'infelicities' or occasional maladroit phrasing, the resort to the Miltonic high style has not only been 'redeemed' but may also have contributed to the story's spiritual momentum.

The novel's symphonic compass moves freely between registers of style, from the empyrean of literary and the clay of spoken English, varying into a carefully modulated lyricism which makes it possible to read *Wuthering Heights* as poetry. From the wilderness poetry of the sublime ('Heathcliff is...an unreclaimed creature...an arid wilderness of furze and whinstone...he's a fierce, pitiless, wolfish man'), where character is terrain, Emily Brontë effortlessly modulates to the beautiful. The beautiful is generally known when you are *not there*. The moors are hardly described at all in the first half of the novel: they are the numinous realm beyond, off the page in the unconscious mind.

The 'handful of golden crocuses' Edgar brings to the dying Cathy are a memorial of her lost native land, the 'earliest flowers at the Heights... They remind me of soft thaw winds, and warm sunshine, and nearly melted snow': the vista called up in absence breathes out on waves of memory, evoking life-restoring cyclical processes. The beautiful is always vestigial, belonging to memory, wish, or presentiment. It is never experienced as the here and now. As the dying Cathy sits in the open window, she seems to gaze 'out of this world': 'the full, mellow flow of the beck in the valley came soothingly on the ear' (*WH* 156). Verbal music mesmerizes, as the 'l' sounds in 'full' and 'mellow' lap and lull into the rhyme of 'flow': but this trance is not the real thing. It is, says Nelly, 'a sweet substitute for the yet absent murmur of the summer foliage, which drowned their music about the Grange when the trees were in leaf' (*WH* 157). This (absent) soughing is a minor echo of major 'wuthering'. But neither would this be the real thing. Indeed, it cancels it out, for 'At Wuthering Heights it [the beck] always sounded on quiet days, following a great thaw, or a season of steady rain': beauty is a reminder of exile. The author is so sparing with her lyricism in the first half of the novel that it seems to subsist in clefts in the rock, like those fragile harebells of which Emily and Anne were so fond. In the second half of the novel, the orchestration is fuller and freer, with a Schubertian outpouring of melody (and with a correspondent loss, perhaps, of the Beethoven-like turbulent depths of the first half). The second Cathy expresses her heart's desire to lie in a 'rustling green tree' amidst multitudinous birdsong:

> a west wind blowing, and bright, white clouds flitting rapidly above...and the moors seen at a distance, broken into cool dusky dells; but close by, great swells of long grass undulating in waves to the breeze; and woods and sounding water, and the whole world awake and wild with joy. (*WH* 248)

Internal rhyme (*bright, white*... *dells, swells*), and alliteration (*west wind, white, waves, woods, water, world, awake, wild*) plays in the key of 'W' a kinesis of exultation. Yet, oddly, the effect is less powerful than the sparing earlier glimpses. The second Cathy's presentation of her dreamscape is aestheticized into a painterly view and a divertimento of birdsong, whereas her mother's was a spiritual experience of being in nature, beyond any words save pure symbol. Ironically, Linton Heathcliff's rival dream of drowsing all a summer's day 'in the middle of the moors' is just as close to (and as far from) her mother's and his father's inhabiting of joint private space. The dream divides here: Cathy Linton wakes up, Linton Heathcliff drops off. The aura of bare, unaccommodated vision is lost, in elaboration on the one hand and torpor on the other. But this movement towards conscious-ness is essential to the resolution of the novel: like the recapitulation of the classic sonata form, the novel re-presents its original themes as reveries rather than deep dream in order to complete its pattern. Catherine and Hareton, 'C' and 'H', will marry in the same key but without the discords of the original Catherine and Heathcliff.

Early reviews ventured tentative suggestions that *Wuthering Heights* was influenced by the literary renaissance of the German *Märchen*, or folk tale:

> His work is singularly original. It bears a resemblance to some of those irregular German tales in which the writers, giving the reins to their fancy, represent personages as swayed and impelled to evil by supernatural influences. But they give spiritual identity to evil impulses, while Mr. Bell more naturally shows them as the natural offspring of the unregulated heart.[15]

The reviewer shows insight in insisting on the *natural*-supernaturalism of *Wuthering Heights*. Emily Brontë sets up a field of two-way suggestion in which the demonic is located both in the animal and the spiritual worlds. If dogs are friends, if pain is hellish, if malediction and its synonyms (curse, execration) are a staple of speech, this is hell-on-earth. But the moorland lyricism also implies the near existence of heaven-on-earth. The drama of the novel inhabits a middle realm between heaven and hell. Readers come away feeling that they have encountered something of cosmic moment. The persona of the novel consider their choices and actions as a drama not of personalities but of souls. Good church-going Anglicans might wear their souls on their sleeves as a Sundays-only custom, for best. The common person – exemplified by Nelly – despite a superstitious quirk or two, esteeming herself 'a sensible sort of body', does not experience herself as a 'soul' every minute of every day.

But the Heights characters are obsessively soul-conscious, from Joseph to Hindley. Suspended on a demonic continuum between heaven and hell, the 'H' characters go 'to the devil' as spectacularly as possible, blaspheming all the way. They dedicate themselves to this soul-business so ardently as to pluck the phrase 'going to the devil' out of the realm of metaphor. Fratricidal in relation to one another (Hindley versus Heathcliff), the hellraisers are Byronically parricidal in relation to God. Infernal antics prevail. Sodden Hindley proudly relates his achievements in upending the doctor in the bog; calls for scissors to shear his lad's ears ('Damn thee, kiss me!'); and assures Nelly he will have 'great pleasure in sending [my soul] to perdition to punish its maker.... Here's to its hearty damnation!' (*WH* 75). His oath, 'By Heaven and Hell' implies there's nothing to choose between the pair of them. Joseph graphically describes Heathcliff's helpful and athletic efforts to speed Hindley down the 'broad high way that leadeth to destruction' in gaming, drinking, and destroying himself: Hindley 'gallops dahn t'Broad road, while [Heathcliff] flees afore tuh oppen t'pikes' (*WH* 104).

The infernal drone of Joseph's services in the garret, where the child congregation is condemned to bide three mortal hours 'on a sack of corn, groaning and shivering' (*WH* 18), is their hell. A retributive God who has pre-damned the reprobate and pre-elected the saved is represented by Joseph, figure of the

Dissenting hypocrite, despised by the whole Brontë family, from father to youngest daughter. A book in Patrick's collection called *An Earnest Address to the Working Classes of Old England... By A Poor Man*: has been endorsed by Patrick in ink on the title-page: 'This work is just & excellent, in all its parts.' The passionate Tory Anglicanism of the earnest addresser stigmatizes 'the glaring inconsistency, hypocrisy, and cant of our various dissenting brotherhoods'. He describes a Bedlam of contrary sects, produced by individual conscience, from Congregationalism, Wesleyans, 'a new edition of popery', Quakers, Ranters who 'rant, and rave, and roar like a bedlamite let loose', Socinians, Swedenborgians, followers of 'old dame Joanna Southcote', bearded like goats. Dissenters are 'common disturbers', gabbling 'everlasting cant... lying hypocrites'.[16] Emily's Joseph is a centre of disorder. In Lockwood's revelatory first dream, Joseph guides the dreamer to Jabes Branderham's outrageous sermon 'divided into *four hundred and ninety* parts', in which the unforgivable sinner is to be 'publicly exposed and excommunicated' (*WH* 21). Lockwood and Branderham denounce one another as reprobate – one as tyrannical bore, and the other as profane fidget, and the service climaxes in a fiesta of mayhem in which 'Each man's hand was against his neighbour' (*WH* 22). God's house is a madhouse, a site of saturnalian conflict in which nothing is sure but uproar, outrage, and the tyranny of pious talkers. As sole representative of the Christian Deity in *Wuthering Heights*, Joseph stands in for the Almighty and comes in for mockery all round. Meanwhile, the church at Gimmerton quietly falls down – a kind of clearance operation on the part of mother nature. Each time we see it, the church has yielded to the moorlands.

In line from Scott's dialect-speaking Scottish retainers, Joseph grafts his religion to place, earth, working farm, hearth, garret, daily round. He eternally fills his baccy pipe, rebukes Nelly's ballads as 'glories to Sattan', fumes against womankind, laments his gooseberry bushes, and is immortally viewed as a late vignette, as he 'solemnly spread his large Bible on the table, and overlaid it with dirty bank-notes from his pocket-book' (*WH* 315), the deliberative *solemnity* of this act giving the laying of lucre on the holy book a ritual air. Fixated on others' sins, Joseph acknowledges none of his own, as he stomps about his master's and his Master's callings.

The credal passion of Joseph is matched – and reversed – by the credal passion of Catherine and Heathcliff. His hell is their idea of heaven; his God their bane; his devil just a chip off the old block; and his Bible is a scribbling pad for a girl's profane testament. His idea of sin is their notion of blessedness; his church their anathema. Yet the lovers, just as much as Joseph, have a sense of the holy, of communion and excommunication. They understand a moral law and embrace with impassioned conviction a set of values. Locating their blessedness in forbidden territory, their home is in transgression and their God is their union. Catherine and Heathcliff are 'heathens' who belong to heath and earth, hearth and heart rather than heaven.

What they account blessed is contained within the cryptic mirrors of the Heights characters' riddling names, which are near-synonyms:

CATHERINE:	HEAT[H]	EARTH	HEART[H]	HEAT[H]EN	HEART	HEAT	EARN– – –	HARET-N
HEATHCLIFF:	HEATH	EA–TH	HEA–TH		HEA–T	HEAT	CATHE-I- -	
EARNSHAW:		EAR–H	HEAR– –		HEAR–	HEA–		
HARETON:	HEAT-	EARTH	HEART-	HEAT- –N	HEART	HEAT	EARN- H – –	

In this recycling of a series of significant letters, we catch glimmering intimations of an obsessive inward drive which compels the Heights characters towards their affinities rather than their opposites, homing to kin in earth where the keywords EARTH, HEART, HEAT, HEARTH are all pledges of sanctuary. Further, the characters' names contain one another: most of HARETON and the HEATH of Heathcliff is contained in CATHERINE. Two-thirds of CATHERINE is contained in the word HEATHCLIFF. All three names burn with HEAT and home to HEARTH. These fugitive bondings in the very names of the characters affine them to EARTH, their source and destination; their holy ground. They are near-namesakes. The soul on these heights is self-licensing, choosing the wilderness into which God drove Adam and Eve in Genesis, as against the pallid Eden or hypocritical heaven in which they cannot belong.

Cathy's dream of ejection from heaven is our first token of her spiritual affinity. Pitched from a *heaven* which was not her *home*, the rebellious Cathy breaks her *heart* to return to *earth* in the middle of the *heath*. God's heaven would be exile, as the comfort of marriage at Thrushcross Grange will be alienation from home and self. Names are self-affirmations in *Wuthering Heights*: forsaking her maiden name, Earnshaw, for burial in a stranger's name, as exogamous patriarchal societies expect women to do, is projected as a nightmare loss of self. Heathcliff, who has no real surname (sire's name), stands outside the patriarchal order in parity with Catherine and all women. For him, Catherine is always 'Catherine Earnshaw'. The second generation returns a second Catherine to the original surname. In taking a stranger's name, the first Catherine knows 'In whichever place the soul lives – in my soul, and in my heart, I'm convinced I'm wrong!' (*WH* 79), and she strikes with one hand her forehead, with the other her breast. Early loyalty in the Emily Brontë universe is as paramount in *Wuthering Heights* as it had been in Gondal:

> But that pure light, changeless and strong,
> Cherished and watched and nursed so long,
> That love that first its glory gave
> Shall be my pole star to the grave.
>
> ('Now trust a heart that trusts in you' (1837))

Where fidelity to the soul's original bearings is primary, other considerations of ethics and theology are reversed. Catherine and Heathcliff recognize a binding principle of right and wrong, but primarily in relation to one another. They see nothing wrong in their conduct to others. An antinomian code of ethics repudiates considerations of '*duty* and *humanity!* ... *pity* and *charity!*' in Heathcliff's sneer at Linton's kind care of his wife. Though he abides by the legal code (for expedient reasons), Heathcliff despises the law of God and man, acknowledging only Catherine's will as sovereign over his. Although *Wuthering Heights* does not ask us to accept this barbarous standard, it honours its sublime excess. Edgar Linton's more-than-motherly gentleness is movingly presented; his forbearance and strength, and the longevity of his love, are accorded respect. Nevertheless, the vital and deadly soul-passion of like for like, which challenges social and Christian values, centres the novel.

Cathy's death punishes what both regard as 'wrong-doing'. At their last meeting, Heathcliff taunts her as the unforgivable sinner. She is 'damned':

'... *Why* did you despise me? *Why* did you betray your own heart,

Cathy? I have not one word of comfort – you deserve this. You have killed yourself. Yes, you may kiss me, and cry; and wring out my kisses and tears. They'll blight you – they'll damn you. You loved me – then what *right* had you to leave me? What right – answer me – for the poor fancy you felt for Linton? Because misery, and degradation, and death, and nothing that God or Satan could inflict, would have parted us, *you* of your own will, did it...would *you* like to live with your soul in the grave?'

'Let me alone. Let me alone,' sobbed Catherine. 'If I've done wrong, I'm dying for it. It is enough! You left me too; but I won't upbraid you! I forgive you. Forgive me!' (WH 161)

Remorseless emphases: *Why...why..right..you...you...you*, stab at the dying Catherine with the accusation of breaking a sacred bond of faith. Gored love discharges itself as rage. For the heretical lovers, the unforgivable sin is to cause 'parting', which belongs to a cluster of keywords expressing trauma, *parting, desertion, stranger, separation*. Catherine acknowledges her trespass, and her 'I forgive you. Forgive me!' asks atonement for the breaking of a bond mutually understood as holy. *Wuthering Heights* carries Romantic metaphor (the identity of lovers) into the literal and spiritual spheres. The transference is initially made by stealthy sleight of hand, almost below the level of our consciousness, as when Nelly describes the sundered children (Heathcliff being locked in the garret) as 'hold[ing] communion through the boards'.

In the second part of the novel, Heathcliff carries the burden of a man who is a ghost of himself before he is dead. An obsessed shadow seeks its vanished substance, in the form of a body toiling through time after a shade which had fled into Eternity. Heathcliff tracks, against all reason, his original counterpart; a relict in a world which has become a mocking reliquary. He finds traces of her in her portrait, and especially in the memorializing and tormenting eyes of her daughter and namesake, and her nephew, Hareton. Sleepless, monomaniac, finally fasting and electric with manic joy as he hallucinates (or sees? the text is not telling) his soul's desire, Heathcliff continues faithful in his integrity: 'To-day, I am within sight of my heaven – I have my eyes on it', adding and believing that 'as to repenting of my injustices, I've done no injustice, and I repent of nothing' (WH 328, 333).

While it is possible to read this as a statement of the legitimate revenge of the dispossessed underclass, appropriating the property of the class which has exploited him, goods and chattels are always seen in *Wuthering Heights* as secondary to love and sustenance. Heathcliff's accumulation of wealth is compensatory. The fratricidal struggle between Hindley and Heathcliff as boys expresses an underlying rivalry for paternal preference. The bond between Catherine and Heathcliff covers for and replicates the all-sustaining mother-bond each lacks. Heathcliff's elaborate design to grasp the Grange and Heights estates through intimidation, fraud, arranged marriage, and brutalization is a compensatory drive to substitute for the magnitude of inner loss.

I have used the word 'relict' to describe Heathcliff's status after Catherine's death. A relict was a word deep-rooted in patriarchal dynastic tradition whereby, since women were covered in law by their husbands, having no independent existence, they became subsequent posthumous leftovers. In a woman, the posture of Heathcliff would have been reactionary. An extreme of this custom was the Hindu *suttee*, the practice of widow-burning on her husband's pyre, a popular discussion topic of the 1820s–1840s, and a subject pondered in Letitia Landon's *The Inprovisatrice* (1824).[17] *Blackwood's* and other journals ran reports of widow-sacrifice, which fascinated Charlotte Brontë, who wrote an arresting essay for M. Heger entitled 'Sacrifice of an Indian Woman', in which the narrator describes step by step the ritual of voluntary sacrifice by which the widow follows her husband into death:

> I thought she was going to renounce the sacrifice; I hoped so; but no, either pride or religion sustained her to the end. She sat down close to the corpse, which had already been laid on the pyre. Then she turned her head to bid the world farewell.
>
> Never in my life will I forget that moment; her eyes sought the sun, the azure sky – I thought I saw in their gaze an agonising struggle between bodily weakness and spiritual power. (*BE* 5–7)

The attitude is complex: feminist and Western aversion from barbarity, recognition that woman-burning is only an extreme version of Western misogyny, together with awe at self-immolating courage greeted as sublime.

Emily Brontë's contrary vision imagined a *male* 'covered' by a woman; a man committing the equivalent of *suttee*. Behaviour which in a widow would have appeared an extreme variation on a norm took on manic or demonic strangeness when attributed to a man. The sublimity of Heathcliff's dead-alive quest for a woman whose loss annihilates him is achieved by imagining what is unimaginable in a patriarchal society. Grafting this reversal on to a behaviour culturally gendered 'male' (violence, rapacity, mercenariness, rebellion against the social and divine order – all impulses she knew in herself), the author covers her trail. Emily Brontë laughs in the face of all gender-codes.

Milton figured hell as ravenous. No matter how many souls it devoured, it could never begin to fill its craving need. *Wuthering Heights* ends in an irony of total engrossment and equally total famine. Having licked up both Linton and Earnshaw heirs, Heathcliff sees the irrelevance of the engorgement he has achieved. His 'fingers relaxed' on the second Catherine, and he 'gazed intently on her face', seeing there a picture of her mother, and finding his thirst not only unslaked but intensified by the fulfilment of his avaricious plans. It is as if the second Catherine stands as a daguerreotype of the first, a reproduction in both senses of a lost original. The shadow of the first, her lineaments and expressions remind him of the loss and brand its extent upon his memory (for her face memorializes Catherine's marriage with Linton), bereaving him of all volition. The second Catherine is not just a picture but a biological remnant of her mother, rather in the sense that Susan Sontag notes of photographs. Their images, she says are

> able to usurp reality because first of all a photograph is not only an image (as a painting is an image), an interpretation of the real; it is also a trace, something directly stencilled off the real, like a footprint or a death mask.. a photograph is never less than the registering of an emanation (light waves reflected by objects) – a material vestige of its subject in a way that no painting can be.[18]

The idea of a 'trace', 'material vestige' of a lost original is haunting and luminous for readers who track Heathcliff as his eyes track Catherine in *Wuthering Heights*. The likeness which he finds in the second Catherine is as abhorrent as blasphemy to the righteous, a perfect quotation in the mouth of a delinquent. Focusing on the mirroring eyes of Catherine and Hareton, he loses his impulse to blight their future, as if they had only the status of shadows on the surface of reality. His thirst is not only unslaked but intensified by the fulfilment of his avaricious plans.

It is now that Heathcliff stops eating mortal food, feeling 'a strange change approaching'. This has been compared with that change which precedes death in terminal illness: but the phrase has apocalyptic suggestions, reverberating from Paul's first letter to the Corinthians:

> Behold, I shew you a mystery; We shall not all sleep, but we shall all be changed.
>
> In a moment, in the twinkling of an eye, at the last trump: for the trumpet shall sound, and the dead shall be raised incorruptible, and we shall be changed.
>
> For the corruptible must put on incorruption, and this mortal must put on immortality....
>
> O death, where is thy sting? O grave, where is thy victory? (15:51–6)

Heathcliff gazes upon a heathen counterpart to this mystery, in which reproductions of one woman's being come to fill the entire field of vision. The concluding chapters chart Heathcliff's apostate revelation, after years of prayer to the godforsaken image of a God-defying girl. Heathcliff's dedication to 'one universal idea' is an idolatrous perversion of the mystic's devotion, a spiritual drive to the truth of a Catherine who exists (so his faith leads him to believe) beyond the surfaces that mirror but belie her: 'I have a single wish and my whole being and faculties are yearning to attain it,' he says, gazing into a universe which has now become, under stress of desire, nothing in itself but only a surface which acts as a screen or glass, onto which his desire projects endless mirrorings of Catherine:

> for what is not connected with her to me? and what does not recall her? I cannot look down to this floor, but her features are shaped on the flags! In every cloud, in every tree – filling the air at night, and caught by glimpses in every object by day, I am surrounded by her image! The most ordinary faces of men and women – my own features – mock me with a resemblance. The entire world is a dreadful collection of memoranda that she did exist, and that I have lost her!' (WH 324)

Heathcliff's mind has turned into a camera lucida which

projects a teeming multiplicity of photographic reproductions upon the face of external reality, which is steadily being abolished as a thing-in-itself. It exists solely as a surface to reflect his inner contents, which are poured out upon creation. A twist on the Berkeleyan logic that said the sun and moon existed only in the eye of the beholder makes the beholder able to abolish sun and moon as real to him, and copy upon their surfaces his mind's reality: an infinite sequence of Catherines. All these briefly 'glimpsed' Catherines act as mnemonics, like a photograph album to the bereaved, of her one-time existence and her perpetual absence. Daguerre claimed for his invention that 'the DAGUERREOTYPE is not merely an instrument which serves to draw Nature; on the contrary it is a chemical and physical process which gives her the power to reproduce herself'.[19] For Heathcliff, whose truth is in the eye of the beholder, Catherine seems to be 'showing herself'; spectral behaviour fully in keeping with the caprice which was her character before she became a spectre. Eerily, Ernest Renan, giving a modern focus on Plato's Ideas, thought that 'The daguerreotypes of all things are preserved... the imprints of all that has existed alive, spread out through the diverse zones of infinite space.'[20] In an age fascinated and unsettled by the new possibilities of image reproduction, surface could now be imagined as visionary.

For Heathcliff, whose trauma of separation and self-division issues in the tragedy of an endless multiplicity of images of the one beloved, his 'one universal idea...a single wish' towards which his 'whole being and faculties are yearning' awaits the moment when this disparity of being will unite in a single image, with which he may in turn close. This is the apocalyptic 'change' he envisages. The longing for oneness is echoed in *one*, *single*, *whole*. Nearing 'the final bound' of his pilgrimage, his body quivers 'as a tight-stretched cord vibrates – a strong thrilling, rather than trembling', Nelly notes (*WH* 328); 'My soul's bliss kills my body but does not satisfy itself.' The author's imagery implies pre-orgasmic tension held at unbearable length. Far from the asexual novel critics used to proclaim it, *Wuthering Heights* speaks of a language of the spirit in terms of acute (but nightmarishly chronic) sexual arousal. Nelly notices that 'he breathed as fast as a cat' (*WH* 327). As the dispersed images

116

lingeringly resolve into one figure, he lays his life aside, 'I am within sight of my heaven – I have my eyes on it – hardly three feet to sever me!' (*WH* 328). Intense desire halts his breathing for half a minute, and his face betrays 'pleasure and pain, in exquisite extremes', as the phantasmal appearance kindles without satisfying his urgent desire. Exultation in the eyes of the corpse at the lattice where the Cathy-spirit had first appeared to Lockwood implies a penultimate surge of joy as he springs from mortal to immortal planes.

Praying 'like a methodist', Isabella sneered at Heathcliff's supplications for Catherine's return as his bereavement commenced. Never a truer word was spoken in gall. Joseph's tabernacle is Heathcliff's hell. Heathcliff's holy of holies is Joseph's anathema, and, when 'Th'divil's harried off his soul', 'the old sinner' mimes his death-grin: 'I thought he intended to cut a caper round the bed,' Nelly recalls.

The query on the validity of the surface of the world we know, or think we know, around us, remains to the end. Lockwood's snowscape, mocking the eye with capricious undulations, gives way to the daguerreotypic play of surfaces on to which Heathcliff's imagination plays out phantasmal images of loss. Catherine, not Heathcliff, is the dominant partner in the pairing: yet, curiously, it is Heathcliff who has emerged as the popular 'hero' of *Wuthering Heights*. 'Be content, you always followed me,' says Catherine in her delirium (*WH* 127), a reminiscence but also a prolepsis, for Heathcliff will 'follow' Catherine through the next eighteen years covered by the remainder of the novel, in quest of a boundary between time and eternity, where living and dead might commune. In the second half of the novel, it is the magnetized rather than the invisible magnet that calls us. In relation to the communal world, Heathcliff behaves like an automaton as he diligently searches for that way through, dealing out punches and kicks to his victims as he goes. He resembles a machine programmed to produce destruction. Given this round of violence, what causes us to be moved by Heathcliff?

A pathfinder, he explores at the limits of human need and desire. On the verge of instinctual animal life; on the uplands of insentient nature where 'the eternal rocks' meet heathlands and storm; at the graveside looking death in the face, he moves, like

Goethe's Faust, Byron's Manfred, to the threshold of 'this world'. Seen as beyond the human – dog, wolf, cuckoo, rock, heath, storm, demon – he has also been shown as an orphaned and ill-used child to whom belongs the reader's sympathy. The search for Catherine runs along the same eye-beam as Emily Brontë's poetry, in waking dreams which 'kill me with desire':

> Then dawns the Invisible, the Unseen its truth reveals;
> My outward sense is gone, my inward essence feels –
> Its wings are almost free, its home, its harbour found;
> Measuring the gulf it stoops and dares the final bound!
>
> ('Julian M. and A. G. Rochelle' (1845))

The poem's disappointed ecstasy records the entombment of the eye in the finite body, the here and now. The visionary poems record intense but baffled curiosity about 'the Invisible', the 'Unseen', represented in *Wuthering Heights* by the dead Catherine. Readers thrill to Heathcliff because he excites, more than any other character, our own curiosity. As he backtracks to Catherine, with straining eyes, so readers track his search. 'The first and simplest emotion which we discover in the human mind,' said Burke, in *On the Sublime and the Beautiful*, 'is curiosity... curiosity blends itself more or less with all our passions.'[21]

And what happened next? is every child's question. *Wuthering Heights* leads us into a state of curiosity which is conclusively inconclusive. The country folk think Heathcliff walks; Nelly wobbles on the subject of ghosts – 'I believe the dead are at peace, but it is not right to speak of them with levity'; Lockwood, passing the kirk which is reverting to nature, satisfies us with a reflective reverie that affirms nothing, while it allows words to bury themselves in 'that quiet earth'. Desire remains unfulfilled; the book perpetuates its mystery.

118

Notes

CHAPTER 1. A QUESTION OF PRIVACY

1. I am indebted to Ann Dinsdale, Assistant Librarian at the BPM, for this information.
2. PB, 'The Irish Cabin', *Cottage Poems* (Halifax, 1811), 69.
3. 'The Happy Cottagers', ibid, 21.
4. John Milton, *Paradise Lost*, I. 589–91.
5. CB, letter to EN, 16 Feb. 1850, in MS Grolier, E17, fos. 4–5, BPM.
6. MB, 'The Advantages of Poverty in Religious Concerns', n.d., MS, fos. 1–2, Brotherton Collection, Brotherton Library, University of Leeds, W. Yorkshire.
7. PB, letter to John Buckworth, 27 Nov. 1821; Elizabeth Gaskell, letter to Catherine Winkworth, 25 Aug. 1850, LG 124.
8. CB, letter to W. S. Williams, 31 July 1848, LFC ii. 241.
9. Quoted in H. and A. Gernsheim, *A Concise History of Photography* (London, 1971 edn.), 64.
10. 'Photography', BEM CCCXVIII (Apr. 1842), vol. LI, pp. 517–18.
11. CB, letter to W. S. Williams, 2 Nov. 1848, LFC ii. 269.
12. John Greenwood's 'Diary', BPM.
13. CB, letter to EN, 7 Aug. 1841, L. 266.
14. Hannah More, *Moral Sketches of Prevailing Opinions and Manners...* (London, 1819). BPM copy, acquired by PB in 1820, pp. 70, 166–7, 295.
15. Laetitia Wheelwright to Clement Shorter, Jan. 1896, quoted in Joseph Green, 'The Brontë–Wheelwright Friendship' (1915), typescript, i. 23
16. A. M. F. Robinson, *Emily Brontë*, (London, 1883), 48.
17. EN, 'Reminiscences', reprinted in L. 598–9.
18. EN's collection of sheet music (1830), p. 11, stanzas 1, 3.
19. William Carus Wilson, *The Children's Friend for the Year 1824* (Kirkby Lonsdale, 1824), 211–12, BPM (SB: 2906); *The Children's Friend for the Year 1826* (Kirkby Lonsdale, 1826), 28, 237, 147–53, BPM (SB: 1351).

20. CB, letter to W. S. Williams, 15 Feb. 1848, *LFC*, ii. 189.
21. T. W. Reid, 'The Brontë Novels: *Wuthering Heights*', in *CH* 400.
22. As quoted by Irene Cooper Willis in *The Authorship of 'Wuthering Heights'* (London, 1936), 14.
23. CB, 'Biographical Notice of Ellis and Acton Bell', *WH* 365.
24. See Victoria Fattorini, 'Early Nineteenth Century Cooking in Haworth', in *The Brontë Society and the Gaskell Society Joint Conference Papers* (Haworth, 1990), 88.
25. CB, letter to EN, 9 Aug. 1854, *LFC* iv. 145; G. 400; CB, letter to EN, 20 Oct. 1854, *LFC* 155.
26. *A New and Easy Guide to the Pronunciation and Spelling of the French Language* by Mr. TOCQUOT (London, 1806), BPM (SB: 1338).
27. Dr Butler's *Classical Geography... A Sketch of Modern and Ancient Geography, for the use of Schools*, incorporates *A Grammar of General Geography... By the Reverend J. GOLDSMITH (London, 1823), BPM. See blank pages and inside covers.
28. George Allan, *Life of Sir Walter Scott* (n.p., 1834), BPM (SB: 1222), *passim*.

CHAPTER 2. 'THE WELL-SPRING OF OTHER MINDS': WHAT EMILY KNEW

1. *The Musical Library*, vol. III Vocal (n.p.); BPM (1131/3), (emphasis added).
2. See Robert K. Wallace, 'Emily Brontë and Music: Haworth, Brussels and Beethoven', *BST* 18/2 (1982), 136–42.
3. George Eliot, *Middlemarch*, ed. W. J. Harvey (Harmondsworth, 1965), 190.
4. George Eliot, *Daniel Deronda*, ed. Barbara Hardy (Harmondsworth, 1967), 299.
5. *The Musical Library*, vol. IV Instrumental (n.p.), Preface of March 1837, BPM (1131/4).
6. George Allan, *Life of Sir Walter Scott* (n.p., 1834), 63–5.
7. Stevie Davies, *Emily Brontë: Heretic* (London, 1994), 51 (emphasis added).
8. Rabenhorst's *Pocket Dictionary of the German and English Languages*, part 1 (London, 1843), BPM (SB: 257); Schiller's *Sämmtliche Werke*, vol. i. (Stuttgart u. Tubingen, 1838), BPM (SB: 2141).
9. J. Rowbotham, *Deutsches Lesebuch; or, Lessons in German Literature...* (2nd edn., London, 1837), 287–8, BPM (SB: 1222).
10. 'The Poems and Ballads of Schiller', *BEM* CCCXIII (Sept. 1842), vol. LII, 285.

11. 'Cassandra'. *BEM* CCCXXV (Nov. 1842), vol. LII, 569–76.
12. Lord Byron, *Manfred*, II. iv. 117–49, in *The Poetical Works* (London, 1966).
13. Felicia Hemans, 'A Spirit's Return', in *Songs of the Affections* (1830), in *The Poetical Works* (London, n.d.).
14. 'Frederick Schlegel', *BEM* CCCXXXV (Sept. 1843), vol. LIV, 324.
15. CB, letter to W. S. Williams, 15 Feb. 1848, *LFC* ii. 189.
16. CB, 'Editor's Preface to the New Edition of *Wuthering Heights*', (London, 1850) 369.
17. AB, *Agnes Grey*, ed. R. Inglefield and Hilda Marsden (Oxford, 1991), 44, 45.
18. *BE*, 176–9. I have silently amended Sue Lonoff's translation where I judge it inauthentic.
19. Charles Darwin, 'E' Notebook, in Howard E. Gruber, *Darwin on Man: A Psychological Study of Scientific Creativity, together with Darwin's Early and Unpublished Notebooks*, ed. Paul Barrett (London, 1974), 460.
20. Henry Vaughan, 'The Book', in *The Complete Poems*, ed. Alan Rudrum (Harmondsworth, rev. edn., 1983).
21. 'Berkeley and Idealism', *BEM*, CCCXX, June 1842, vol. LI, 817.
22. Ibid. 818, 819.
23. Ibid. 821.
24. 'Some Remarks on Schiller's *Maid of Orleans*, *BEM* CCCXLVI (Aug. 1844), vol. LVI, p. 217.
25. PB, *The Phenomenon, or, An Account in Verse, of the Extraordinary Destruction of a Bog...* (Bradford, 1824), 4–5.
26. Ibid. 9.
27. Edmund Burke, *A Philosophical Inquiry into the Sublime and the Beautiful* (London, 1827 edn.). The provenance of this volume is unsure: it was said to have belonged to CB. BPM (SB: 2436).
28. C. P. Sanger, *The Structure of 'Wuthering Heights'* (London, 1926).
29. CB, 'The Search after Happiness', 17 Aug. 1829. See Winifred Gérin, *Charlotte Brontë: The Evolution of Genius* (London: 1967), 43 ff., for the treatment of John Martin.
30. Sir Humphrey Davy, *Elements of Chemical Philosophy* (London, 1812), BPM (SB: 419).
31. Ibid. 1, 27–8, 29, 98, 103.
32. Stevie Davies, *Emily Brontë* (Brighton, 1988), ch. 3.
33. *Richard Baxter and Margaret Charlton: A Puritan Love-Story*, being *The Breviate of Margaret Charlton* by Richard Baxter, ed. J. T. Wilkinson (London, 1928), 80.

CHAPTER 3. THE HOUSE OF TRAUMA: A READING OF *WUTHERING HEIGHTS*

1. Amy Tan, *The Hundred Secret Senses* (London, 1996), 26.
2. e.g., Herbert Dingle, *The Mind of Emily Brontë* (London, 1974).
3. Terry Eagleton, Editor's Preface to James H. Kavanagh, *Emily Brontë* (Oxford, 1985), p. xii.
4. J. Hillis Miller, '*Wuthering Heights*: Repetition and the Uncanny', in *Fiction and Repetition in Seven English Novels* (Oxford, 1982), 43–71.
5. *Wutheringshöhe*, trans. anon (3 vols., Grima and Leipzig, 1851), iii.
6. *Sturmhöhe*, trans. Ingrid Rein (Stuttgart, 1986), 433.
7. *Die Sturmhöhe*, trans. Ingrid Rambach (Germany, 1938).
8. *Hurlement*, trans. Sylvère Monod (Paris, 1963), 471.
9. Novalis, *Schriften*, ed. Richard Samuel *et al.* (Stuttgart, 1960–75), 35–6.
10. Alfred Lord Tennyson, 'In Memoriam A. H. H.', section LIV, in *Poems and Plays* (London: Oxford University Press, 1965).
11. Friedrich Schlegel, 'Literary Aphorisms', in *'Dialogue on Poetry' and 'Literary Aphorisms'*, trans. Ernst Behler and Roman Struc (University Park, Pa., and London, 1968), 131–2.
12. CB, *Young Men's Magazine* (Oct. 1830). See Edward Chitham, *A Life of Emily Brontë* (Oxford, 1987), 60–1.
13. Ibid. 54.
14. G. W. Peck, unsigned review of WH in *American Review*, 7 (June 1848), 572–85, in CH 235–7.
15. Unsigned review of WH in *Britannia* (15 Jan, 1848), CH 223.
16. *An Earnest Address to the Working Classes of Old England, On the Aims and Objects of the Religious and Political Parties of the Day, By A Poor Man* (London, 1836), 123–6, 136, BPM (SB: 1309).
17. See Isobel Armstrong, *Victorian Poetry: Poetry, Poetics and Politics* (London, 1993), 318–47.
18. Susan Sontag, 'The Image World', in *On Photography* (New York, 1977), 154.
19. Louis Daguerre, 'Daguerreotype', in *Classic Essays on Photography*, ed. A. Trachtenburg (New Haven, Conn., 1980), 13.
20. Quoted in Sontag, *On Photography*, 202.
21. Edmund Burke, *A Philosophical Inquiry into the Sublime and the Beautiful* (London, 1827 edn.), 25–6.

Select Bibliography

WORKS BY EMILY BRONTË, HER SISTERS AND MRS GASKELL

Emily Brontë, *The Complete Poems of Emily Jane Brontë*, ed. C. W. Hatfield (New York: Columbia University Press, 1941).

—— *Emily Jane Brontë: The Complete Poems*, ed. Janet Gezari (Harmondsworth: Penguin, 1992).

—— *The Poems of Emily Brontë*, ed. D. Roper and E. Chitham (Oxford: Oxford University Press, 1994).

—— *Wuthering Heights*, ed. Ian Jack, with an introduction by Patsy Stoneman (Worlds Classics; Oxford: Oxford University Press, 1995).

Charlotte Brontë and Emily Brontë, *The Belgian Essays*, ed. and trans. Sue Lonoff (New Haven, Conn.: Yale University Press, 1996).

Anne Brontë, *Agnes Grey*, ed. R. Inglefield and Hilda Marsden (Worlds Classics; Oxford: Oxford University Press, 1991).

The Letters of Charlotte Brontë, i. *1829–47*, ed. Margaret Smith (Oxford: Clarendon Press, 1996).

The Lives, Friendships and Correspondence of the Brontë Family, ed. T. J. Wise and A. Symington (4 vols.; Shakespeare Head; Oxford: Basil Blackwell, 1933).

Elizabeth Gaskell, *The Life of Charlotte Brontë*, ed. Alan Shelston (Harmondsworth: Penguin, 1975).

—— *The Letters*, ed. J. A. V. Chapple and A. Pollard (Manchester: Manchester University Press, 1966).

BIOGRAPHICAL STUDIES OF EMILY BRONTË AND HER FAMILY

Barker, Juliet, *The Brontës* (London: Weidenfeld & Nicolson, 1994). A monumental work of scholarship, historically reliable, attractively and clearly written, though lacking in feminist and literary awareness, and dedicated to normalizing the Brontë family, especially through rehabilitation of the Brontë menfolk.

Chitham, Edward, *A Life of Emily Brontë* (Oxford: Basil Blackwell, 1987). Sensitively and scrupulously written, attentive to every scrap of evidence, this is a scholarly and sympathetic introduction to EB's life and work.

Gordon, Lyndall, *Charlotte Brontë: A Passionate Life* (London: Chatto & Windus, 1994). Superbly written account of CB which sheds light on EB's life and work by emphasizing the tension between them.

CRITICAL WORKS

Allott, Miriam (ed.), *The Brontës: The Critical Heritage* (London: Routledge & Kegan Paul, 1974). Well-edited compilation of nineteenth century reviews and critical statements concerning the Brontës.

Armstrong, Isobel, *Victorian Poetry: Poetry, Poetics and Politics* (London: Routledge & Kegan Paul, 1993). A magisterial volume, beautifully written, in which women poets are placed within and against their age's cultural perspective.

Davies, Stevie, *Emily Brontë* (Harvester Women Writers Series; Brighton: Harvester, 1988) Offers discussion of EB's 'sinistral' vision, using -handedness theory as a liberating alternative to psychoanalytic approach; attempts a strong engagement with EB's language.

——— *Emily Brontë: Heretic* (London: The Women's Press, 1994). Sets out a feminist case for EB as a well-read dialectical thinker in the tradition of German Romantic philosophy, with anti-Christian and -patriarchal alignment and pro-animal sympathies.

Eagleton, Terry, *Myths of Power: A Marxist Study of the Brontës* (Basingstoke: Macmillan, 1975). This ground-breaking study suffers by its placement of Heathcliff at the centre of *Wuthering Heights*, turning it into a patriarchal text. The author has since recanted on this point.

Gilbert, Sandra and Gubar, Susan, *The Madwoman in the Attic: The Woman Writer and the Nineteenth-Century Imagination* (New Haven, Conn.: Yale University Press, 1978). Brilliant analysis of anti-patriarchal inversion of theology made by EB; questionable but stimulating reading of women writers as suffering from 'anxiety of influence'.

Hillis Miller, J., 'Wuthering Heights: Repetition and the Uncanny', in *Fiction and Repetition in Seven English Novels* (Cambridge, Mass.: Harvard University Press, 1982), 43-71. Accessible and profound reading of *Wuthering Heights* defining the novel as an uncanny text which compels but prohibits interpretation.

Jacobs, Naomi, 'Gender and the Layered Narrative in *Wuthering Heights* and *The Tenant of Wildfell Hall*', *Journal of Narrative Technique*, 16 (1986), 204–8. Argues that the male violence of the 'central' story is endorsed by the 'civilized' outer structure.

Kavanagh, James, *Emily Brontë* (Basil Blackwell, Rereading Literature Series; Oxford: 1985). Hysterical dance of psycho-sexual/Marxist/poststructuralist/bearded feminist enthusiast, which is successful in its attempt to obscure the novel. The worst excess Theory has (yet) produced.

Kermode, Frank, '*Wuthering Heights* as Classic', in *The Classic* (London: Faber & Faber, 1975). Exciting seminal essay which was one of the first to accept the 'plurality' of readings.

Leighton, Angela, *Victorian Women Poets: A Critical Reader* (Oxford: Blackwell, 1996). Discerning collection of essays which create a sophisticated sense of context in which to place EB.

Pykett, Lyn, *Emily Brontë* (Macmillan Women Writers Series; Basingstoke: Macmillan, 1989). A wise, carefully wrought, jargon-free feminist reading of EB's life and work.

Stoneman, Patsy, *Brontë Transformations: The Cultural Dissemination of 'Jane Eyre' and 'Wuthering Heights'* (London: Prentice Hall, Harvester, 1996). Encyclopaedic and analytic account of CB's and EB's work as it has entered into and been transformed by the culture, in film, novels, theatre, criticism, opera, illustrations, magazine stories and other iconography.

—— (ed.), *Wuthering Heights* (Macmillan New Casebook Series; Basingstoke: 1993). Presents a choice gathering of the newest writing on EB, in the light of Marxist, feminist, psychoanalytic, structuralist, and poststructuralist theory; exemplary introduction.

Index

Recent and
Forthcoming Titles
in the
New Series of

WRITERS AND
THEIR WORK

RECENT & FORTHCOMING TITLES

TITLES IN PREPARATION

Title	Author
Antony and Cleopatra	Ken Parker
Jane Austen	Meenakshi Mukherjee
Alan Ayckbourn	Michael Holt
J.G. Ballard	Michel Delville
Samuel Beckett	Keir Elam
William Blake	John Beer
Elizabeth Bowen	Maud Ellmann
Charlotte Brontë	Sally Shuttleworth
Caroline Dramatists	Julie Sanders
Daniel Defoe	Jim Rigney
Charles Dickens	Rod Mengham
Carol Ann Duffy	Deryn Rees Jones
E.M. Forster	Nicholas Royle
Brian Friel	Geraldine Higgins
The *Gawain* Poetry	John Burrow
Gothic Literature	Emma Clery
Henry IV	Peter Bogdanov
Henrik Ibsen	Sally Ledger
Geoffrey Hill	Andrew Roberts
Kazuo Ishiguro	Cynthia Wong
Ben Jonson	Anthony Johnson
Julius Caesar	Mary Hamer
John Keats	Kelvin Everest
Rudyard Kipling	Jan Montefiore
Charles and Mary Lamb	Michael Baron
Langland: *Piers Plowman*	Claire Marshall
C.S. Lewis	William Gray
Katherine Mansfield	Helen Haywood
Measure for Measure	Kate Chedgzoy
Vladimir Nabokov	Neil Cornwell
Old English Verse	Graham Holderness
Alexander Pope	Pat Rogers
Dennis Potter	Derek Paget
Lord Rochester	Germaine Greer
Christina Rossetti	Kathryn Burlinson
Mary Shelley	Catherine Sharrock
P.B. Shelley	Paul Hamilton
Stevie Smith	Alison Light
Wole Soyinka	Mpalive Msiska
Laurence Sterne	Manfred Pfister
Tom Stoppard	Nicholas Cadden
The Tempest	Gordon McMullan
Charles Tomlinson	Tim Clark
Anthony Trollope	Andrew Sanders
Derek Walcott	Stewart Brown
John Webster	Thomas Sorge
Mary Wollstonecraft	Jane Moore
Women Romantic Poets	Anne Janowitz
Women Writers of the 17th Century	Ramona Wray
William Wordsworth	Nicholas Roe